Lonely Walk

The Life of SENATOR
MARK
HATFIELD

Robert Eells & Bartell Nyberg

CHRISTIAN HERALD BOOKS
Chappaqua, New York

We acknowledge with appreciation permission to quote from:
Between a Rock and a Hard Place by Mark O. Hatfield. Word Inc., 1976.
Conflict and Conscience by Mark O. Hatfield. Word Inc., 1971.
Not Quite So Simple by Mark O. Hatfield. Harper and Row, 1968.
"The Illusion of Arms Control" (interview) *Sojourners* magazine, February 1979.
"On Power and Responsibility" (interview) *Vanguard* magazine, April 1976.

Library of Congress Cataloging in Publication Data

Eells, Robert.
    Lonely walk.

    Bibliography: p.
    Includes index.
    1. Hatfield, Mark O., 1922–   2. Christianity and politics.   3. United States — Politics and government — 1945–   4. Legislators — United States — Biography.   5. United States. Congress. Senate — Biography.   6. Baptists — United States — Biography.   I. Nyberg, Bartell, joint author.   II. Title.
E840.8.H3E34   973.92′092′4 [B]   79-50942
ISBN 0-915684-49-7

To Dr. Walter E. Eells
father, supporter, friend

Contents

Preface   9

1. "Ratting on America"   13
2. Beginnings   19
3. Peeling Back the Veneer   27
4. A Growing Christian Faith   35
5. Oregon's Political Enigma   41
6. On the Threshold   49
7. Radicalization Begins: Vietnam and the Draft   59
8. The Trouble With Senator Hatfield   71
9. A Prophetic Christian Politics   81
10. "Redoing the System"   99
11. Tweedledee, Tweedledum   113
12. The Beam in Our Eye   123
13. Blessed, and Hungry, Are the Poor   131
14. Vintage Hatfield   145
15. Quo Vadis?   155

Epilogue   171

Appendix: Christian Socio-Political Organizations   175

Notes   185

A Selected Hatfield Bibliography   195

Index   199

Preface

Like many graduate students, I had difficulty choosing a dissertation topic. I discussed several possibilities with my doctoral committee in the American Studies Department at the University of New Mexico. One adviser, knowing of my interest in Christianity and politics, suggested that I write a biography of an evangelical politician. I quickly proposed Sen. Mark O. Hatfield of Oregon as my subject, and the committee responded favorably.

After contacting the senator's Oregon and Washington, D.C. offices in 1974-75, I received permission to begin my research. My wife and I spent several weeks in Oregon before heading east to the nation's capital.

I worked in Hatfield's Washington office for several days without seeing him. I was apprehensive, wondering when that moment would come. One day, as I talked to one of the senator's staff members, I knelt between a desk and the wall to get something from my briefcase.

At that moment, Hatfield entered the room. I stood up, looked him in the eye—and gulped. He smiled, and I blurted out something about being grateful to be in Washington. He shook my hand and left the room.

Moments later Wesley Michaelson, Hatfield's executive assistant, came to see me. Laughing, he said the senator had just told him about meeting the nicest telephone repairman! Michaelson guessed, correctly, that it was me. He left, still smiling.

Soon Hatfield returned. We laughed about our chance meeting, and he invited me to join him for lunch that day. Our relationship started on the right foot after all.

Later, after Michaelson escorted me to the top floor of the

Senate office building to dig through some of Hatfield's records, I reflected on my encounter with the senator. What was I doing there? The temperature outside was 95 degrees and the storage area wasn't air-conditioned. Even after discarding my shirt I was perspiring heavily.

As I rummaged through the boxes, I found all kinds of information—including personal correspondence. What sort of politician, I asked myself, would give a stranger access to such information? Only a secure and trusting man, one who faced the future confidently, I concluded.

That judgment was confirmed as I came to know the senator better. I hope that my dissertation and this revision do justice to this remarkable politician, this *Christian* politician.

Robert J. Eells
May 1979

Acknowledgments

Many people have supported this project, starting with my doctoral committee at the University of New Mexico. The committee director, Dr. Charles Biebel, gave me the freedom to pursue my goal. My dissertation editor, Mrs. Margaret Franke, worked long and hard on the form of the manuscript. Luci Johnson and Rebecca Bustamante typed the dissertation.

Later, Dr. Gene R. Marlatt, academic dean of Rockmont College in suburban Denver, Colorado, encouraged me to revise the dissertation and seek publication. He provided many useful contacts, including the typists (Christine Ireland, Tani Sharp, and Cynthia Foss) for parts of the manuscript.

This book would not have been possible without the significant revision undertaken by Bartell Nyberg, who is a co-author in the truest sense. He not only reconstructed the dissertation manuscript but also did much of the typing and editing at various stages.

Finally, Bart Nyberg joins me in thanking our wives, Janice Eells and Jan Nyberg, for their support. Partners like them made the task much easier.

Lonely Walk

"Ratting on America"

> The trouble with ... Hatfield ... is that he has confused his own philosophy with the true teachings of Jesus. There is a fundamental difference between killing for murder and acting as an agent of God's processes. ... All talk of ending the Indochina war ... before the Communists are stopped is immoral. ...[1]
>
> Letter to *Eternity* magazine

THE YEAR WAS 1966. Despite a fifteenfold increase in United States ground and air forces in 18 months, despite $2 billion a month in U.S. military and economic assistance, and despite official pronouncements to the contrary, U.S. and South Vietnamese armies were not winning the Vietnam War.

Already, placard-waving students throughout the country and abroad—but, as yet, precious few politicians—questioned American intrusion into an Asian war. To counteract such dissent, President Lyndon B. Johnson seized every opportunity for support of his war policy. When the nation's governors gathered in Los Angeles, California, in July 1966 for their annual conference, the president dispatched a "truth squad" to enlist the governors' endorsement.

Administration representatives, headed by Ambassador Averell Harriman, were keenly aware that a year earlier two governors (Mark O. Hatfield of Oregon and George W. Romney of Michigan) had refused to lend such support. After a White House briefing, featuring the president himself, Romney switched to a pro-administration position. Hatfield never withdrew his negative vote.

13

This time the White House wanted no dissenters. "Hanoi knows the names of all those who have been ratting on America," Harriman declared threateningly, pointing his finger at the governors assembled in the Century Plaza Hotel.[2]

Eager to avoid the political consequences of "ratting on America," and perhaps also eager to sop the presidential ego, Democratic governors quickly prepared a resolution of support:

> Whereas, the purpose and intent of bipartisan American foreign policy . . . is a search for peace and stability with honor . . . be it resolved that this conference affirm to the President, the American public, the service men and women . . . its resolute support of our global commitments, including our support of the military defense of South Vietnam against aggression.

As he had a year earlier, Governor Hatfield sought clarification of the term "global commitments." He received none. Hatfield then proposed an amendment offering support only for American fighting men in Vietnam; it was voted down.

Texas Gov. John Connally, a longtime presidential crony, told his fellow governors that their only "patriotic" choice was to vote for the original resolution. Several governors urged Hatfield to "get lost" for a few minutes—for his own political good—while the vote was taken. Rejecting the advice, the Oregon governor remained to cast his vote. He described the scene in his book *Not Quite So Simple:*

> One after the other the "aye" votes sounded in the hushed room. As the roll call came nearer . . . the room began to seem to me like one vast sound chamber with the "ayes" pounding monotonously against the wall. . . .
>
> My wife Antoinette was in the room, sharing the moment of trial. As in a dream I could see the photographers methodically manipulating their cameras, making ready to close in on me. The room was enormously quiet when Oregon was called. I did not know how I would sound when the moment came to answer. I found my voice and said "No." My "No" was neither mean nor bitter nor antagonistic. It was simply "No."

> It was all over then. . . . When the vote was tallied, as the
> whole room well knew, the result was 49-1 in favor. . . .[3]

When Oregonians arose the next morning, they were greeted with newspaper headlines like "Mark 1, Others 49 on Vietnam War Policy." Some editorial writers called the governor's action "courageous," others termed it "disgraceful." As a whole, media reaction was unfavorable.

Since Hatfield already had announced his candidacy for the U.S. Senate in the 1966 election, most observers called him a political fool for his vote. Peter Gunnar, chairman of Oregon's Republican Party, openly disapproved of Hatfield's stand.

Time magazine (October 14, 1966) observed that the "immediate result of Hatfield's antiwar stand was . . . to bring Democratic Representative Robert Duncan charging into the senatorial race" for the seat of retiring Democrat Maurine Neuberger. Duncan firmly supported the president's war policy.

Though the polls indicated Hatfield was in serious trouble because of his dovish position, he refused to compromise. To avoid being trapped in a one-issue campaign, he tried to emphasize economic matters. That tactic was only partially successful, for Duncan aggressively kept the focus on Vietnam. If we don't fight the Communists "in the elephant grass of Southeast Asia, then we will have to fight them in the rye grass of the Columbia River Basin," Duncan charged.[4]

Senator Wayne Morse of Oregon, a liberal antiwar Democrat, did Hatfield no favor when he announced he would support the Republican governor rather than Duncan. To differentiate his views from those of Morse, Hatfield opposed unilateral withdrawal from Vietnam and refused to attack the president personally. Still, Hatfield did not back down. His position was courageous because—aside from Morse and a handful of others—it was a lonely point of view to take during this initial phase of U.S. military involvement in Vietnam.

Few observers were aware of the personal crisis, both spiritual and political, in Hatfield's life during this crucial election campaign. Some critics contended that Hatfield's blend of liberal

politics and evangelical religion was a fraud, that Hatfield attempted the impossible by fusing liberal politics with "Baptist piety." In
the eyes of evangelicals, he tackled the impossible by doing the
reverse:

"[Hatfield] works both sides of the street," the *Portland Oregonian* (July 5, 1974) quoted an anonymous source. "One Sunday he
will give us as liberal speech as you will want and the next Sunday
will come out with a fundamentalist talk." Some evangelical leaders quietly approached Hatfield and accused him of being a
"stumbling block" to other Christians because of the anti-American
appearance of his Vietnam position.[5]

As Hatfield recalls the conflict, two opposing forces confronted
him:

> There was a growing question in my mind. If I [was] in God's
> will, I had to stop programming my life so far ahead. I had
> myself programmed for every campaign for the next ten,
> fifteen years. Now, if [winning those elections] is God's will,
> I have to trust him for it. . . .
>
> Then, from the other force, was the growing political
> circumstances that were developing, saying you're
> through. . . . This is it! Cut and run! So, from the spiritual
> and from the political, I was caught in this inexorable eye.

Hatfield didn't cut and run. He continued to raise serious questions about Vietnam. In making his political peace with God, he
said he was willing to accept defeat in the election and continue his
fight for peace elsewhere.

"I had the closest shave of my whole career," Hatfield says. "But
after the votes were counted, I had to assume it was God's will that
I was to be there." In a Republican year, Hatfield collected 354,000
votes, Duncan 330,000.

Hatfield felt his victory signified God's will that he not only
continue his opposition to the war but also continue to spell out the
political implications of his Christian faith. That crucial watershed
experience speeded Hatfield's metamorphosis toward a more radical evangelical perspective on both political and spiritual issues.

Who is this man who professes a personal faith in the saving blood of Jesus Christ—and yet could oppose not only the president of the United States but also the bulk of the American evangelical establishment?

Who is this man who claims that Jesus is Lord—and yet refused to discourage Oregon's state colleges from allowing American Communist leader Gus Hall to speak on campus?

Who is this man who circulates in the traditionally conservative circles of Baptist congregations—and yet could be an early voice for the extension of civil rights to blacks and other minorities?

Who is this man who nominated Richard Nixon for president at the 1960 Republican National Convention—and yet could be listed among the president's enemies a dozen years later?

Beginnings

> I never can recall as a youngster when I wasn't somehow involved in politics. And there was no question in my mind that ultimately I wanted to become engaged in political action of a candidate character.

THE HEART OF OREGON—its population, its agricultural bounty, its governmental and educational institutions, its pioneer heritage, its economy—is the broad Willamette Valley and the timbered slopes of the bordering mountain ranges.

It was here that Jason and Daniel Lee established a Methodist mission outpost in 1834, about the time that mountain men from the Rocky Mountains arrived in quest of furs. And it was tales of rich Willamette soil that prompted thousands of pioneers in Conestoga wagons to brave the dangers of the Oregon Trail in the 1840s.

In this valley Mark Odom Hatfield was born July 12, 1922. His home was in Dallas, a town of just 2,701 persons.

Charles Dolen (C. D.) Hatfield, the boy's father, was a construction blacksmith for the Southern Pacific Railroad. Young Mark's grandfather also had been a blacksmith and wainwright in Indiana before seeking new opportunity in the West. Despite the physical demands of his work, C. D. Hatfield was a kind, quiet, gentle man. For years he taught Sunday-school classes and directed Sunday-school singing in Dallas's Baptist community. He was a soft-spoken Democrat.

Mark's mother, Dovie Odom Hatfield, was born in the hill country of eastern Tennessee, where allegiance to the Republican Party was *the* way of life. Mrs. Hatfield's mother named her "Dovie" after a doll-like midget she had seen in a traveling show.[1] When Mark was just five, his mother placed her son and husband

19

under the temporary care of Grandma Odom and went off to college. Four years later, in the midst of the Great Depression, she graduated from Oregon State College (now University) at Corvallis, thirty-two miles from Dallas.

Mrs. Hatfield taught school in Dallas for two years. Then she found a job in a Salem junior high school, where she taught for thirteen years. Even though the move from Dallas to Salem was short, just twelve miles, the change may have been vital to Mark Hatfield's political development. Salem, the state capital and seat of Marion County, was a Republican stronghold.

Mark's father was a devoutly religious man. He saw to it that the Hatfields were nearly always among the faithful who gathered on Sundays and Wednesday evenings to hear the pastor's sermons. Young Mark dutifully sat through these sermons, which were frequently illustrated with complicated charts and graphs. Rebellion was not an ingredient of the boy's personality; he gave no sign of questioning this conservative Baptist perspective.

Mark was an only child. His parents delighted in dressing the boy in his Sunday best so that he might attract the attention of admiring adults after the services. In these early years the boy did nothing to detract from his image as almost a young dandy. Before long, no doubt, he accepted such public attention as normal.

During Hatfield's childhood and adolescence, most Oregon Baptists clung to a rigid philosophy of church/state separation. The spiritual dimension of life had priority, and the institutional church was the proper place to demonstrate one's spirituality. Despite this separatist view, however, Mark became involved in politics at an early age.

This involvement can be explained by parental ambition, largely maternal. While the boy's father was the spiritual pillar, his mother was more influential in shaping Mark's social and political awareness. She was a staunch Republican, had a dominating personality, and wanted her son to succeed in the world. She wanted him to receive the best possible education—one that would qualify him for some form of public service.

At age ten Mark hauled Herbert Hoover campaign propaganda around his neighborhood in a coaster wagon. Though he eventually developed a deep admiration for Hoover, that early political activity likely reflected more of his mother's enthusiasm than his own.

By his early teen years, Hatfield developed a strong interest in local Republican and school politics. He frequently attended local political rallies and met campaign trains at the railroad station. In his first try for elective office—student body president in junior high school—he defeated a formidable opponent: Shirley McKay, daughter of Douglas McKay, then mayor of Salem, later Oregon's governor, and still later secretary of the interior under President Dwight Eisenhower.

There is evidence that the adolescent Hatfield already recognized he was working against the grain of his fellow church members. Leolyn Barnett, who was secretary to five Oregon governors, including Hatfield, recalls how even as a teenager he occasionally confronted church leaders with pleas for Christian involvement in the world. His arguments at times were sufficiently forceful to prompt the raising of a few elderly eyebrows.

Although there was little suggestion of open hostility, the church leaders apparently didn't know what to think of this young man. Eventually, their resistance to Hatfield's social and political perspective cooled the youth's passion for institutional Christianity. He gradually realized that for many believers Christianity meant only an all-encompassing relationship with the institutional church.

Believing that his perspective was true to Scripture, Hatfield began to drift away from the institutional church. By his late teens and early twenties, he exhibited signs of rebellion. The rebellion was mild by modern standards, but he did flout some conventional mores. For instance, sometimes he blew pipe smoke into his clothing before departing for church—so that some of the older women would be sure to smell the evidence!

The waning of his interest in the institutional church was matched by a waxing of his interest in politics. One event in the late 1930s greatly affected young Hatfield, then a high school student: U.S. Postmaster General James A. Farley's address at the dedication of Salem's new post office. Hatfield, age fifteen, played the clarinet in the Salem High School band at the ceremony.

Democrat Farley impressed the young Republican first by presenting his speech in a steady rain, then by shaking hands with all who tarried in the audience. Next Farley turned to the band, thanking each bandsman for his efforts despite the weather. That wasn't all; after Farley returned to Washington, he sent a personal letter of appreciation to each band member.

Inspired by Farley's example, Hatfield soon found work weekends and summers as a guide for tourists in the new state capitol. He also handled odd jobs for Earl Snell, then secretary of state.

After graduating from Salem High in 1940, Hatfield enrolled in Willamette University, a Methodist school in Salem. It was there that he lost an election for president of the student body, the only loss of his career. Hatfield majored in political science, taking just three years to complete work on his degree. Shortly after graduation, the U.S. Navy summoned him to active duty. After completing amphibious training, he was assigned to an attack cargo ship in the Pacific war zone.

Before World War II, Hatfield had a two-pronged political philosophy: (1) isolationism and (2) opposition to President Franklin D. Roosevelt. His isolationism was probably due to the natural inclination of many young men to keep America out of any developing European conflict. His opposition to FDR was also predictable, given the political bent of Marion County.

Isolationism proved to be the more short-lived portion of his philosophy. His first doubts about isolationist policies emerged about 1940, after exposure to Wendell Willkie, whom the Republicans nominated to oppose FDR in the 1940 presidential election. Longtime U.S. Senator Charles L. McNary—a native of Marion County—was nominated to be Willkie's vice-presidential running mate. Willkie, a Democrat-turned-Republican, had long preached the need for international cooperation.

World War II destroyed any vestiges of isolationism in Hatfield—and further affirmed some of his doubts about institutional Christianity. As a landing-craft officer (and unofficial chaplain) in the Pacific theater, Hatfield confronted situations far unlike the peaceful surroundings of the Willamette Valley.

His landing craft carried troops ashore and evacuated the wounded at Iwo Jima and Okinawa; despite heavy casualties around him, Hatfield escaped injury. In retrospect, he says, it was the war that

> brought me very close to death. . . . It gave me a perspective of life being but a vapor: You see it and you don't see it. . . . The fact that I was sort of an acting chaplain aboard our ship gave me an understanding . . . that the Christian faith was something more than a formal worship service; it was very personal and something very individual. I think that out of that war experience of being close to death I gained two major perspectives—learning the dimension of eternity versus the transitory character of human life, and [learning about] the personal relationships it tended to develop.

In his book *Between a Rock and a Hard Place*, Hatfield relates how his Navy duty "sensitized" him "to the untold suffering of humanity's hungry and poor masses of people." One experience created an indelible impression on his mind:

> I was with a Navy contingent who were among the first Americans to enter Hiroshima after the atomic bomb had been dropped. Sensing in that utter devastation the full inhumanity and horror of modern war's violence, I began then to question whether there could be any virtue in war.[2]

Fourteen years later Hatfield could say that God spared his life in combat "apparently for something he had for me to do in the days ahead."[3] In wartime, though, he found it difficult to relate institutional Christianity to his growing concern for social issues and the potential for a new international order.

Because neither the church nor individual Christians addressed these problems, Hatfield turned to arenas where they might be discussed—notably, the academic community and Republican politics. Still, he didn't cut himself completely away from the church. As a young man searching for a meaningful relationship between his Christian faith and everyday life, he remained in touch with his Baptist community.

Since the war introduced Hatfield to the need for the rule of law at the international level, he enrolled in the Willamette University Law School after being discharged from the Navy. It took him only a few months, however, to decide that he really wanted to teach political science or run for public office, or both.

Thus, in 1947 Hatfield entered Stanford University's graduate program in political science. He chose Stanford because it housed the Herbert Hoover library; it was to Hoover that Hatfield turned in his quest for personal and political fulfillment.

Hoover was a logical choice for someone seeking a moral base for political action. As a practicing Quaker, Hoover had spent a lifetime trying to work out the implications of Quaker Christianity for public policy questions. Only in Hoover, and to some extent in Abraham Lincoln, did Hatfield find what he felt were the major emphases sorely lacking among conservative Christians: social concern and a political ethic.

Hatfield's additional study of such European thinkers as John Locke and John Stuart Mill confirmed the political philosophy he found in Hoover. Hatfield was impressed with the stress all three put on the individual, individual self-government, and ideas of limited government. He was also exposed, however, to the modern idealism of Wendell Willkie and Thomas Dewey. Their idealism implied a more positive view of the state than was characteristic of classical liberalism (including its modern expression in Hoover). Only a more mature Hatfield would attempt to resolve these apparently contradictory political philosophies.

At Stanford Hatfield was elected to the governing student council as a write-in candidate. That taste of politics whetted his appetite for a more active political role. He and his friend, Travis Cross, an undergraduate student and fellow Navy veteran from Salem, discussed the possibility of Hatfield running for political office in Oregon.

After completing work on his master's degree, which included a thesis on Hoover, Hatfield accepted an offer from his friend, President G. Herbert Smith of Willamette University, to teach political science. At the same time, Smith hired Cross as Williamette's director of information.

Hatfield quickly moved into the political arena. Within one year, he was chairman of the Young Republican Policy Committee in Oregon and Marion County's chairman of the National Citizens Committee for the Hoover Report on executive reform. As a final step, the young teacher sought to integrate education and politics by seeking public office. In the fall of 1950 he was elected to the legislature as a Republican representative from Marion County.

Hatfield's political acumen was apparent even in that first campaign:

> There was nothing of Joe College then, or later, about his campaigning. He hit every dusty road and dusty hamlet; he sought advice from weekly newspaper editors and from laboring men; he was unwearying. In the Republican primary there were twelve candidates for four legislative posts; Hatfield topped the ticket in the primary and in the general election.[4]

He was the first college teacher to serve in the Oregon legislature in more than thirty years. At twenty-eight, he was the youngest legislator. And, no doubt, he was one of the few bachelor legislators still living at home with his parents.

Conveniently, the capitol was located just across State Street from Willamette University. Hatfield and President Smith worked out a reduced teaching schedule enabling the new legislator to concentrate his classes in the 8:00-10:00 a.m. slot. After completing his second class at 9:50 a.m., Hatfield could dash across the street in time for the 10:00 a.m. opening gavel at the legislature.

The Cross-Hatfield political express was on the move in the Willamette Valley.

Peeling Back the Veneer

The number one thing that Mark Hatfield did is that he changed loyalties—from self to Christ.

Douglas Coe

IN THE EARLY 1950s Hatfield was concerned primarily with his own political future, not the integration of faith with politics. Dovie Hatfield's determination had created, or at least nurtured, a deep emotional need for public service and acclaim within her son's psyche. And Hatfield considered himself the ideal young politician: a man of principle and integrity, perfectly suited for public office because he was obligated to no one.

Today, some political observers consider Hatfield lucky. Others call him an astute opportunist. Some Christians believe him a man chosen by God. Whatever one's explanation, Hatfield early logged a record of choosing the "right" side. For example, he was one of the first—in February 1951—to urge publicly that Republicans draft General Dwight D. Eisenhower as their 1952 presidential candidate. In July 1951, Hatfield started circulating petitions to place Eisenhower's name on the Oregon presidential primary ballot. That early groundwork paid off. For the first time Hatfield was noticed in national political circles. A year later he headed the Oregon Citizens for Eisenhower organization.

Taking the lead on Eisenhower's behalf paid another dividend. Hatfield was elected a delegate to the Republican National Convention. Oregon Republicans selected Hatfield over U.S. Sen. Wayne Morse for the state's important post on the convention's platform committee. At the convention Hatfield gained first-hand exposure to national Republican leaders.

Before long, Hatfield's political ambition began to trouble some Oregonians. His early support for Eisenhower was seen as a self-serving power play by one observer: "Hatfield impresses me as an extremely eager, ambitious young man who would rack his brain for any idea to accomplish his goal."[1]

Unlike many politicians, however, Hatfield began to recognize the ego problems associated with political ambition, especially as they related to his spiritual life: "All of these honors were highly encouraging. . . . But with the outward advancements came a disturbing inner awareness of my inadequacy in the area of the spiritual life."[2]

Hatfield's growing spiritual uneasiness reached crisis proportions about 1953. Formal identification with Christianity "was too automatic. It was a religion of habit, not of commitment."[3] Even a somewhat lukewarm identification with institutional Christianity allowed him to drift along comfortably, but it didn't provide the answers for the difficult questions he faced.

The most disturbing questions came from students at Willamette University. After his first year of teaching, Hatfield was promoted to dean of students. Thus, it was natural for troubled students to come to him for answers:

> . . . some of my students began to ask me questions that involved their own personal lives like Who am I? What's life? Who is God? . . . those were pretty basic questions. You couldn't get a political science answer to that kind of question. . . .
>
> They began to get very specific in this. I was driven more to generalities by their increased specificity. . . . I would refer them to, "Well, now what's your denomination? Why don't you go down and talk to Rev. Brooks? He's the kind of guy you should talk to."

Dodging these penetrating questions troubled Hatfield. It dawned on him that he had little to offer spiritually to these students. "I began to realize," he says, "that I was everything spiritually that most of my students were politically. I was as a-spiritual as they were a-political."

Strangely, help came from other students—a group of evangelicals whose lives showed evidence of spiritual fullness. Hatfield unobtrusively observed these students at every opportunity. He found their selfless attitude so appealing that he developed a casual friendship with Douglas Coe, one of the group's leaders. Coe, in turn, sought to make the "conversion" of Mark Hatfield a priority among the evangelical students.

Coe and others suggested that Hatfield read certain parts of Scripture for help in answering the disturbing questions from other students. Hatfield found the beginnings of an answer in the Book of Job:

> I was fascinated by that poor man, and I began to realize what it was that kept Job in that complete submission. And then as Job rose victorious out of the ashes, the Lord really spoke to my heart, and I said, "Look, what do you really have to say to these kids? You don't really have much!" But Job had the answer to every single interrogation.

Hatfield believed that Job had an answer because of his unconditional commitment to serve God—a commitment which gave him a basis of self-knowledge and knowledge of the world. Hatfield wanted such knowledge. One evening in 1953 (Hatfield is uncertain of the exact date), alone in his room in his parents' home, he resolved the crisis:

> That night . . . the choice was suddenly made clear. I could not continue to drift along. . . . Either Christ was God, and Savior, and Lord, or He wasn't, and if He were, then He had to have all my time, my devotion, all of my life.
>
> I saw that for thirty-one years I had lived for self and decided I wanted to live the rest of my life only for Jesus Christ.[4]

But what kind of decision was it? It was personal: "I did not sense any immediate need to go out and shout from the housetops. . ." Hatfield recalls. "I saw no reason to publicize the matter."

It was epistemological: The decision provided him with a theological self-knowledge, he says, "a special perspective inside that meant I started on God's terms and not mine." That new perspective allowed Hatfield to begin viewing the church not as an institution but as a body of individual believers.

It was evolutionary in the transformation of his personality and perspective:

> I didn't rise from my knees and say, "Here I am, ready to charge forth." I was not sure that what I had done was right. I thought, "Gee, maybe I'll wake up in the morning and say I've made an ass of myself. . . . But before I got up the next morning I had a reaffirmation of what I had done the night before.

In response to Coe's invitations, Hatfield—reluctantly at first—began speaking to Christian groups about his new commitment. He concentrated on such theological themes as recovering the vision of the early (noninstitutional) church and the desperate need for a spiritual renaissance in America, especially among individuals.

On the one hand, Hatfield's conversion seems to have reinforced his conviction of America's "spiritual" foundation. For him, there continued to be a "deep spiritual recognition undergirding the American political scene,"[5] a type of civil religion in which the political status quo somehow is blessed in the name of Christianity. Closely allied with Hatfield's own brand of civil religion was his application of traditional Christian morality to his view of politics. He looked with favor upon honesty, decency, and truthfulness, with disfavor upon gambling, drinking, and smoking. The young legislator consumed an occasional social cocktail and had smoked for several years; he gave up both indulgences.

On the other hand, following his conversion Hatfield rediscovered a neglected principle of Herbert Hoover—compassion. Compassion soon developed into the integrating link between Hatfield's faith and his politics:

> I became compassionate, more authentically compassionate. I distinguished for the first time in my life between compassion that was based on more of a paternalism and more of a pity, which in itself is dehumanizing [and] a new perspective of. . ."love—compassion."

Paternalism, as exemplified by many modern liberals, seemingly prompts one to care for others as unfortunate objects, not as the deserving recipients of loving concern. Authentic compassion immediately eliminated paternalism as an ethical option for Hatfield.

Many theologically conservative Christians, though, had little interest in Hatfield's developing sense of political ethics. Their overriding concern was not the fact that his position was evolving into progressive Republicanism. The basic issue was "priority," and for them this implied a "spiritual" ministry—one far removed from the mundane world of politics.

Their attitude greatly disturbed the young politician. "I didn't *want* to get out of politics," he says. He was convinced that God had called him to the political arena. For Hatfield, politics was a high calling, too. And he had reason to believe that he belonged in politics. In the fall of 1952 he had been reelected to the Oregon House of Representatives. He won a State Senate seat in 1954. Two years later, in his first try for statewide office, Hatfield was elected secretary of state.

It would have been natural for a young politician with Hatfield's background to move toward the political right. During his early legislative years, McCarthyism made solid inroads into the American consciousness, especially among the more conservative segments of the Republican Party. In the Christian community, those who were conservative theologically tended to be conservative politically.

Hatfield headed in the other direction, toward liberal Republicanism (minus its naive acceptance of the absolute necessity of big government). Liberalism, to Hatfield, has always meant an openness to change and the "ability to put oneself in the position of the other fellow, to evaluate contradictory evidence and look at the many sides of one issue."[6] This kind of openness made Hatfield uneasy with the simplistic approach to politics characteristic of many on the political right.

Concern for others and recognition of the complexity of life emerged in four areas of Hatfield's early political development: education, political reform, civil rights, and extremism.

No doubt because of his academic ties and interests, Hatfield was appointed to the Education Committee of the Oregon House of Representatives. At times he displayed an almost utopian view of the role of education. "Education is the very source of our social being," Hatfield said in 1954. "It is the solution to a greater, stronger, more understanding America." Because parents were preoccupied with other pursuits, he continued, "The educational system has the greater part of the responsibility of teaching Americanism to students and developing citizenship for the future."[7]

While Hatfield suggested that a properly functioning mass education system resulted in a social "salvation," he also recognized that the typical public-school graduate was woefully unprepared for college work. He blamed public schools, as well as parents, for rearing a generation of young people who were unable to understand "relationships" because of an excessive concentration on factual knowledge and artificial categories.

In the area of political reform, one of Hatfield's priorities was to draw up a new constitution to replace Oregon's oft-amended document written in 1859. Little progress was made, and he soon was frustrated by the time required for meaningful change:

> When I first ran for public office . . . and had only my academic training to recommend me, I was prepared in part for some of the obvious hurdles in public life, and especially for public resistance to my age and to my profession. . . . But I was less well prepared in my own mind for the resistance to change which I would find in people, and for the inertia that grips the institutions of government. . . .[8]

Patience was not an easy lesson for Hatfield to learn.

In Oregon, progress in the field of civil rights came somewhat quicker than did political transformation. As chairman of the State and Federal Affairs Committee in the House, Hatfield exerted considerable influence on Oregon's first significant public accommodations bill in 1953. He successfully fought efforts to make approval of the bill dependent upon a public referendum—an approach which he believed would have fanned the flames of bigotry among the voters. Opposing a referendum was a courageous move, particularly in Oregon where citizens long have employed political innovations such as the initiative and referendum.

After the final House vote in favor of the accommodations bill, civil rights supporters joyously proclaimed that Oregon had "banished discrimination" on that day. Hatfield cooled their enthusiasm somewhat:

> "No," I said. "This is not the day."
> They were quiet. Some were surprised, and some were shocked.
> "We have passed a law. We have that law practically within our grasp. But the elimination of discrimination is a constant battle and will not come simply from a law."[9]

Hatfield's approach to political extremism was somewhat ambivalent. He early took a stand against the anti-Communist extremism of the McCarthy years—a position which prompted opponents during one early campaign to accuse Hatfield himself of being a Communist. As a political scientist and public speaker, though, Hatfield frequently spoke against communism. He could defend a scientist like Robert Oppenheimer who was being "subjected to unsubstantiated accusations of political witch-hunters,"[10] but then turn around and recommend legislation requiring teachers to acknowledge past or present Communist connections before they could work in Oregon public schools.

As a state legislator, Hatfield strongly opposed most efforts to centralize political power. He favored a program of decentralized federalism, Republicanism within the two-party framework,[11] a compassionate individualism, and free enterprise.

To Hatfield, decentralization meant localism and regionalism. Individualism meant emphasis upon each person having innate worth. Free enterprise implied democracy and freedom. The two-party system was crucial because it could check the trend toward centralization. At that time, though, many liberals considered centralization the norm. To them, the community good took precedence over the individual (except in civil rights), and some even began to question the free enterprise system. Still, to Hatfield it was entirely logical to be a fiscal conservative supporting decentralized government—and yet call himself a liberal on most other issues. At this time, he successfully integrated the political poles of liberalism and conservatism.

The young state legislator could manage such a balancing act because his liberal programs sought to enhance the well-being of individuals, not to increase the power of government per se. He focused on the legal and humanitarian rights of *individual* Americans. No mention was made of the rights of communities or minorities. Although Hatfield would use government to protect individual rights, he failed to present a view of government where power could be basically good in itself.

Throughout the mid-1950s, when Hatfield's political and religious views were evolving, his popularity climbed considerably in Oregon. In his campaign for secretary of state in 1956, he attracted support from many sources. "He is an excellent representative of the younger, aggressive and enlightened group of Republicans..." the *Portland Oregonian* commented editorially (May 4, 1956). "He would add youth and stature to the Republican ticket."

Many non-Republicans agreed, for Hatfield impressively whipped his Democratic opponent—in an election in which the Republicans lost the governorship and every other statewide office. After conquering his personal spiritual crisis, Mark Hatfield had emerged as a charismatic figure in Oregon politics.

A Growing Christian Faith

> If that inspiration for government comes from Christian principles and Christ-like action, the people will be well served. But if Christians retire to the role of critics of government and reject the opportunities to participate, we shall forfeit our future as a democracy which was founded upon deep religious motivation.[1]

AS HATFIELD SOUGHT to traverse the bumpy political road during his immediate post-conversion years, he encountered two sharply contrasting Protestant approaches to "living in the world." The first posture was that of his childhood Baptist community. "Oh, Brother Mark," several church members told him, "we're so glad to see you squared away with the Lord. Now you'll get out of that horrible slime of politics. . . . God has called you to preach, Brother Mark. We want you to go to seminary. . . ." The other force tugging at the heart of the young politician pulled him in the opposite direction, toward a lifework as a Christian in politics.

Perhaps the best labels for these approaches, at least in the context of the early and mid-1950s, are *fundamentalism* and *evangelicalism*. Precisely what is the difference between a fundamentalist and an evangelical? And where did Hatfield fit during his early years as a state executive in Oregon?

Theologian Harold John Ockenga points out that in matters of basic theology there is solidarity between evangelicals and fundamentalists. Their differences stem primarily from the fundamentalists' belief that no compromise with the world is possible because the world itself is evil. Ockenga defines an evangelical as a Christian

> holding or conformed to what the majority of Protestants regard as the fundamental doctrines of the Gospel, such as

35

the Trinity, the fallen condition of man, Christ's atonement for sin, salvation by faith, not works, and regeneration by the Holy Ghost. [Evangelicals are] in a special sense, spiritually minded and zealous for practical Christian living, distinguished from merely orthodox. . . .[2]

The difference revolves around the phrase "practical Christian living." Ockenga suggests that for evangelicals this denotes compassionate, individual involvement in the world. The same phrase, by implication, tends to pull fundamentalists out of the world.

The evidence clearly indicates that the maturing Hatfield continued to follow the evangelical path during his first years of executive service. This allowed him to appear both orthodox and progressive, theologically.

Hatfield's theological progressivism was evident from his criticism of the institutional church:

I think the reason we [the institutional church] have lost influence . . . is because of our building magnificent edifices and saying, "Here is where God is, come in here if you would find God."[3]

When we fail to appropriate the power and person of Jesus Christ, and to accept Him as Lord and Savior in our total [individual] lives, our religious rites and forms of worship have little meaning.[4]

Despite such criticism, Hatfield's views were tolerated because he was an insider, a member of the evangelical family. He supported such conservative groups as Youth for Christ, Campus Crusade for Christ, and World Vision. He was a board member of the Conservative Baptists' Western Baptist Theological Seminary in Portland, and he made hundreds of presentations to Christian churches and organizations.

In addition, as secretary of state and as governor, Hatfield's personal lifestyle acquired the evangelical stamp of approval. He frequently referred to prayer and Bible reading in public statements, and he practiced what he preached. William Newell, the state police driver for Hatfield during his two terms as governor, relates how Hatfield occasionally would ask him to stop the car so the two of them could pray. The rising politician publicly stated that ". . . the decisions, the policies, and the programs which I follow in my official role I try to root first of all in prayer."[5]

Though he was certainly no political saint,[6] Hatfield frequently exhibited the love and meekness that would be difficult to explain apart from his maturing vision of personal Christian ethics. This is aptly pointed out in an episode which occurred in his successful 1958 gubernatorial campaign.

In an effort to help Gov. Robert Holmes in his campaign against Hatfield, Sen. Wayne Morse—an Oregon Republican-turned-Democrat—resurrected an old tragedy in Hatfield's life. It had happened when Hatfield was just seventeen. One evening about dusk, he was driving the family car along a country road, en route from band practice to pick up his parents at a church picnic. A little girl darted across the road. Hatfield's car hit her and she later died.

Though no criminal charges were filed, the girl's family brought a civil suit against Hatfield's insurance company. Hatfield testified that the girl had been obscured by a mailbox and tall grass; thus, he hadn't seen her until the moment of impact. Nevertheless, the trial court awarded damages.

Morse claimed that the jury hadn't believed Hatfield's story. "A man who lies to a jury cannot be trusted with public office," Morse declared.[7]

That "low blow" backfired. Oregon's former chief justice, who had heard an appeal in the case, and attorneys for the child's parents were among those jumping to Hatfield's defense. They pointed out that there had been no question of anyone lying to the jury.

Hatfield rejected the opportunity to respond in kind. He issued a terse statement regretting the revival of grief for those involved in the incident. Travis Cross, then a political assistant and close friend of Hatfield, recounts that Hatfield exhibited "perhaps the greatest personal witness and biblical admonition of 'turn the other cheek' that I have ever seen in politics." Hatfield, says Cross, treated Morse in a "civil, almost exalted" manner during the few days before and after the election when the controversy was making headlines in Oregon newspapers.

That gubernatorial campaign was also complicated by two other issues with theological ramifications. The first was Hatfield's marriage to Antoinette Kuzmanich, a counselor for women at Portland State College. Miss Kuzmanich, the daughter of a Yugoslav immigrant, was a Roman Catholic until becoming a Baptist the year of her marriage to Hatfield. Both Roman Catholics and Protestants questioned the Baptist-Catholic union. "At that time [the reaction] was vicious, petty, and unconscionable," recalls Cross. A Catholic newspaper refused to carry Hatfield's political advertisements. "By the same token," Cross adds, "the Protestants weren't all jumping for joy. . . . There was great concern about how the children would be raised." Little evidence of that hostility still exists, but for a time both sides exhibited a distasteful display of prejudice.

Ironically, the second issue involved Hatfield's slowly evolving sense of the Christian's individual citizenship responsibility. Two weeks before the election, Governor Holmes accused Hatfield of using "his identification with church activities to get votes. I do not believe in identifying Almighty God with my political party or with any other."[8]

At the time Holmes raised the issue, Hatfield was in Des Moines, Iowa, speaking to the National Sunday School Convention. Hatfield's Oregon staff denounced Holmes' charge as vicious and vindictive. Cross notes, in retrospect, that if Hatfield expected to reap political gain among Oregon evangelicals from a speech, Des Moines hardly would be the place to do it.

Hatfield's response to Holmes was both politically sharp and somewhat disappointing, in light of a more holistic Christian posture: "I do not believe that a man's religious activity should be injected into a campaign."[9] That statement shouldn't be interpreted as hopelessly narrow, however, for even at this early point in his Christian life, Hatfield's politics was more insightful than that pronouncement reflected. About the same time, he also made this comment: "Integration of true Christian living into all areas of life—political, economic, and religious—is imperative for [the Christian] today."[10]

How can one resolve this apparent contradiction in Hatfield's vision of politics? The answer lies in his earlier distinction between two kinds of potential political activity: community activity, under-stood as the institutional church, and individual activity. Hatfield opposed making the church a political organ, but he continued to stress individual involvement by Christians in the political system, warning that apathy would lead to dire consequences.

Admittedly, this still created a considerable distance between Hatfield and his Conservative Baptist community. But in many respects, his practice of and advocacy for individualism and moral-ity in politics moved him towards a limited expression of civil religion. Moral concern led him to ask:

> Are [political] decisions to be turned over to the callous
> hands and warped minds of those who could be motivated by
> selfishness, greed and personal gain? Or shall we insist upon
> character, integrity and ability?"[11]

Reflecting on questions such as these, it is tempting to draw harsh conclusions about the conventional nature of Hatfield's Christian politics during these initial years of public service. But, in fairness, one must keep in mind that he was very much involved, and compassionately so, by evangelical standards. No doubt he was under enormous pressure to be a model Christian public official in the eyes of both evangelicals and citizens at large.

A different perspective was not far beneath the surface. Hatfield was growing in his conviction that the world was crying for help, and that only Christianity had the final solution:

> [Christianity has] the mystic balm that will heal this wound
> of spiritual emptiness and answer this cry for help. We hold
> in our possession the gospel of the Lord Jesus Christ.[12]

Thus, the potential for radical healing is found in Christ, not in American Christianity. In a few short years, Mark Hatfield would move deliberately toward a more thoroughly Christian political philosophy.

Oregon's Political Enigma

> When I was elected governor, I ran against the crown prince of the Republican Party. I ran against the heir apparent... the person touted to be the next Republican candidate for governor.... So the party was very upset with me.... And the resentment was very strong.

MARK HATFIELD was an ambitious young man. He sprinted to the top of Oregon politics in less than a decade. That pace outstripped even Hatfield's own political blueprint, his step-by-step plan to "succeed" politically as his mother had wanted. And as one of two notable Republican survivors—Gov. Nelson Rockefeller of New York was the other—of the GOP massacre in the 1958 election, Hatfield attracted significant attention nationwide. The *Saturday Evening Post* (May 9, 1959) called Hatfield "the new political golden boy of the Pacific Northwest," an "adept, incisive campaigner and a master of the electric smile and the quick handshake."

Still, not all of Oregon's Republican leaders were pleased with Hatfield's sizzling pace and national recognition. "They all thought of me as a young political opportunist... too far, too fast," Hatfield recalls. Some resented his "Mother, God, and country" approach which attempted to fuse politics and evangelicalism.

There was some basis for the old politicians' resentment. Hatfield never had been "one of the boys" hammering out political strategy in the smoke-filled rooms. He had taken on—and whipped—some party favorites en route to becoming Oregon's chief executive. It didn't help when, on the night of his election as governor, Hatfield said: "I want to be Oregon's first two-term governor in this century."

41

Travis Cross explains the leaders' reaction this way:

> Ambition is something an employer wants in a stockroom
> boy. And ambition is something the head of a law firm wants
> in a junior member of the firm. Ambition is something that
> you want of your son when he reaches age seventeen. But,
> for some reason, there are those in the media, and other
> places, who think that ambition in politics is bad.
>
> If Hatfield hadn't been ambitious to be a state representa-
> tive, he never would have made it to that position. If he
> hadn't been ambitious to be a state senator, he wouldn't have
> made it. . . . When Mark was first labeled "not one of the
> boys" was during his legislative period when the lobbyists
> would have big timber parties . . . some of them resulting in
> virtual brawls. Some of my lobbyist friends would say to me,
> "Where's your bookworm tonight—in the library?"
>
> And I would say, "No. He's in your town, speaking to the
> PTA." That's how he built up his following—a 16-hour-a-day
> devotion to work and building a statewide base of friend-
> ship. . . .
>
> Partway through that experience he ceased to drink. He
> ceased to smoke. . . . He's not a backslapper. He's not a
> storyteller. His erect posture and his general manner . . . is
> such that people are either warmed to the tips of their toes
> by his personality and his smile and his sincerity and his
> ability to rivet in one-on-one, eyeball to eyeball.
>
> Or, if they are skeptics or cynics, they go off in a corner
> and put him under a microscope and analyze every hair on
> his head . . . and they are probably jealous of anyone with
> that kind of composure. . . . Fellow politicians are looking at
> his no-lose record and his margins and his Humpty-
> Dumpty, put-it-back-together-again history, and they can't
> quite figure it out.

Looking at Hatfield's record, it is easy to see where opponents
might have considered him an impatient opportunist. Upon taking
office as secretary of state in 1957, Hatfield sought to reorganize the
department—as much as he could do without statute or constitutional change. Then in his inaugural address as governor in 1959,
Hatfield called for massive governmental reorganization "to elimi-

nate the overlapping, the duplications, the inefficiencies. . . . Below the three constitutional and three statutory officials . . . were 89 boards, commissions, committees and councils and 52 other agencies, a total of 141, whose administrators reported directly to the Governor. One man could not possibly keep track of them all."[1]

Hatfield appointed a bipartisan committee, headed by two former Oregon governors, to make specific recommendations on executive reorganization to the legislature. Much to the new governor's satisfaction, the committee called for restructuring state government along the lines of the federal cabinet system. The committee suggested aligning all state agencies under seven departments, each headed by an official appointed by the governor.

Many political observers recognized that such reorganization would greatly increase the governor's power, and they opposed the plan for that reason. They preferred a weak executive and a diffusion of power. Hatfield, however, was convinced that centralization and economy were the only solutions to Oregon's makeshift government:

> We had been primarily a part-time state government. We had a biennial session of the legislature. The governor's office was really sort of a part-time operation. Our state no longer could be governed by part-time operations of citizen commissions.

In 1961 Hatfield and the committee submitted the executive reform plan to the legislature in an all-or-nothing package. In light of Oregon's tradition of individualism and localism, and the resistance of bureaucrats to change, that wholesale approach appears naive. Bureaucratic opposition, Hatfield recalls, proved to be a crucial factor before the legislative committee of inquiry:

> Each agency head or commission member readily conceded. . . that we ought to have reorganization—but his agency should be exempt. . . . We got no reorganization. Looking back, I think we asked for too big a change all at once. For deep inside, and perhaps not so deep, people feel insecure with change. . . .[2]

Hatfield and fellow reform seekers then turned to the piecemeal approach. In 1963 the legislature finally approved one important part—creation of a Department of Commerce. Meanwhile, Hatfield also discovered ways to bring about substantial reorganization without benefit of statute.

Executive reorganization was evidence of a more progressive or liberal Hatfield philosophy, one that was open to change. His reform proposal implied a shift of power from the bottom (local government) toward the top (state government). In the name of economy and efficiency, he proposed merging small governmental units—cities and counties—into larger, more workable organizations.

But wasn't that a contradiction of Hatfield's earlier emphasis on decentralized power? Not entirely. What he opposed was the drift of power toward the federal government: "I felt very strongly that the best way to avoid centralization of power was to have an active, effective state government." In a 1959 speech, Hatfield discussed the rise of national power:

> We are beginning to recognize that there are real disadvantages and not a little danger in the assumption that "Big Brother" government can provide better answers from the banks of the Potomac than we can reach on the banks of the Charles, the Hudson, the Delaware or the Willamette.[3]

Two factors were chiefly responsible for Hatfield's program of reform and a strong state government. First, as secretary of state and later as governor, he viewed Oregon from the angle of an administrator and executive, not of a legislator. As governor, he was confronted with the need to preserve state government from the growing encroachment of Washington. Second, and more important, was his continued reliance upon the philosophy of Herbert Hoover. Once again Hoover proved to be the ideal model for a man seeking to develop a philosophy on power that could fuse liberalism and conservatism.

At least three portions of the Hoover philosophy (as reflected in the Hoover Commission report) influenced Hatfield. First, it gave him a more realistic view of centralized power, both at national and state levels. Second, the philosophy enabled Hatfield to concentrate on executive administration without losing sight of the individual and local government. Third, the philosophy encouraged Hatfield to accept and work within the framework of the American political system.

When he was governor, Hatfield recalls, he was "but an extension of the local community—in a sense, almost acting as their agent, providing state resources to assist them. . . . So, I would say our [administration] was that kind of leadership which recognized and based its philosophy on people being involved through the local community."

The main problem with Hatfield's philosophy of political reform during these years was his assumption that centralized power at the state level was different from power centralized at the national level. He failed to grasp the potential of tyranny at the state level as well as in Washington. According to Hatfield's theory, a strong state government and a strong governor didn't seek power for themselves—only for individual citizens and local governments. Even if Hatfield did fit this mold, others following him in office could hardly be expected to practice such selfless centralization.

Given the nature of Hatfield's political background, and especially the influence of Hoover, it is understandable how the governor's political activity remained a blend of liberalism and conservatism. The conservation issue is a case in point. He backed "responsible" conservation management, an approach allowing legitimate use of natural resources, especially timber. At the same time, Hatfield recognized the views of Oregon's budding environmentalists:

> Whether it was in the area of ecology, environment, economics—we struck the balance. We said, "Look, we need environmental quality, but we need economic growth on a selective basis." We drew them together. We didn't polarize. . . .
>
> In 1955 I was co-sponsor in the State Senate of an air and water pollution bill—the first state in the Union to have air and water pollution criteria. It was in my administration that we took on Portland for pollution of the Willamette River.

Writing in the September 1962 issue of *American Forests*

magazine, Hatfield suggested that "coordinated and harmonious management will, in the long run, increase benefits to all... with proper and coordinated planning, we can have residences and recreation, business and beauty, payrolls and playgrounds." In the same article, Hatfield charged that environmental zealots "who have infiltrated the conservation movement... may so confuse the American public that orderly and wise use of our natural resources is somehow pictured as dishonest and immoral."

Hatfield tilted toward the conservative side in economic philosophy. Although willing to see the state provide certain emergency assistance, he was committed to the free enterprise framework. "The fundamental key to Oregon's success," he said in 1962, "is to make the free enterprise system work and expand."[4]

A stern test for Hatfield's liberal inclinations came near the outset of his first term as governor. A convicted murderer was sentenced to die; as governor, Hatfield was empowered to commute the sentence. He previously had expressed opposition to capital punishment, primarily because of procedural equity ("the rich get off, the poor die") rather than on religious grounds. The voters apparently approved of Hatfield's views, because he had been elected governor by a 60,000-vote margin—in a state with 53,000 more registered Democrats than Republicans.

Yet a short time earlier Oregon's legislature had defeated a measure to repeal capital punishment. If the legislators reflected the will of the electorate, then Oregon's citizens favored the death penalty. The young governor faced an agonizing dilemma. Should he follow his conscience, or should he uphold the will of the people?

> I spent hours in prayer and in deep personal anguish. Finally, I decided that... their will must be honored, notwithstanding the conflict with my personal convictions. So I did not exercise the power to commute his sentence.... There are no doubts in my heart that I reached the most prayerful and responsible decision possible....[5]

As suggested earlier, Hatfield's philosophy of welfare reflected a more liberal viewpoint than that of most Republicans. His was a plea for "disciplined compassion," modeled after the Mormon

Church program: "When in need, help yourself at the common storehouse; when you prosper, help restock the storehouse."

Because of his blend of liberalism and conservatism, Hatfield opposed the Republican Party's drift toward philosophical conservatism. Even in the freer political climate of Oregon, his outspokenness and independence stirred up the party establishment. And Hatfield didn't endear himself to GOP leaders when he avoided the Republican label in the 1958 gubernatorial campaign—precisely so that he would appeal to voters of both parties.

Despite such hostility, by the early 1960s rumors abounded that Hatfield was being groomed for the vice-presidency. Already he had crisscrossed the country on political and religious speaking tours, even delivering the nominating speech for a presidential candidate (Richard Nixon, in 1960). He had taken an active leadership role in the 1961 and 1962 National Governors Conferences. Foes and friends alike recognized that Hatfield was blessed with that special charisma that all politicians want—but few have.

On The Threshold

> As God involved himself in mankind, we must involve our-
> selves in society. We cannot brush aside as inconsequential
> the needs of men, whether they be in poverty, in equal
> rights before the law, or in hunger.[1]

DESPITE GOVERNOR HATFIELD'S growing reputation as a
political maverick, GOP leaders chose him to be the keynote
speaker at the 1964 Republican National Convention. Hatfield's
selection shocked many mainstream Republicans since that was
the year the party nominated Sen. Barry Goldwater, the conservative Arizonan, for president. Just a year earlier Hatfield had in-
vaded Goldwater's hometown, Phoenix, to deliver a stunning de-
nouncement of right-wing political extremism:

> I have no doubt there are men engaged in the fantasies of
> sitting in the White House . . . and engaging in a blood bath
> in carrying out their hate campaigns. [This] would mean the
> literal destruction of the minorities—Jews, Catholics and
> Negroes. I have no time for the extremists' or fanatics'
> right-wing infiltration of the Republican Party. . . . The right
> wing frequently comes under the guise of patriotism and
> [catches] up unthinking adherents.[2]

Why did the Republican hierarchy pick a freethinking West-
erner like Hatfield to make the traditionally unifying keynote
presentation? Did they think the Oregonian wouldn't dare defy the
party line? More likely, pragmatism—Hatfield's charisma, his per-
fect television image and his popularity among Republican governors—overshadowed his liberal shortcomings. *Time* magazine
(June 5, 1964) offered this assessment:

49

> Hatfield (41), a man of boyish good looks, will be responsible
> for whipping delegates into a suitable state of partisan en-
> thusiasm and wooing televiewers to the party cause. . . . His
> delivery is cool, crisp and unemotional. . . . No one doubts
> that the well-tailored, button-down appeal of middle-
> roading Republican Hatfield will be a rating builder.

Choosing a keynoter for his image and not his substance proved to
be an embarrassment to conservative delegates, who nominated
Goldwater in an effort to provide "a choice, not an echo." Hatfield's
address—titled "A Program of Faith"—might have been better
received by Democrats, who were then going through the formal-
ity of nominating President Johnson.

Hatfield delivered remnants of traditionalism in his keynote,
which was not as radical as it could have been:

> We have faith that the American nation and system will
> prevail against the Communist menace that stalks and
> threatens to bury us. . . . We have faith in the free enterprise
> system. . . . And let me remind you that capitalism in the
> United States has brought us to the highest standard of living
> in the history of the world. . . . We have faith in our nation's
> capacity for leadership of the Free World. . . .

To the Goldwater crowd such phrases sounded more like sop
than thoughts from the heart. As he stood before the gathered
thousands—those who would soon boo and jeer when Governor
Rockefeller struggled to defend his own liberal views on civil
rights—Hatfield emphasized a different message:

> We have faith in our capacity to defend human rights against
> the forces of bigotry and hate within our own country. With
> the authors of the Declaration of Independence, we know
> that the rights of men are endowed by their
> Creator. . . . There are bigots in this nation who spew forth
> their venom of hate. They parade under hundreds of labels,
> including the Communist Party, the Ku Klux Klan and the
> John Birch Society.

Hatfield also boldly directed Republicans toward relief for the
elderly and the hungry. He asked for equal opportunities for
minorities in education, employment, and housing. And he fired

one of his first public criticisms at the Democratic administration's handling of the burgeoning war in Southeast Asia:

> Why, why do they fear telling the American people what our foreign policy is? Even when American boys are dying in a war without a name. Tragic as is a tomb for an unknown soldier, still more tragic is the fate of the unknowing soldier, whose life may be lost in a battle the purpose of which he has not been told and which he is not allowed to either win or to conclude.

The crux of the keynote, however, came when Hatfield concluded that the pinnacle of faith for Americans "must be in the strength of our religious heritage and the need for a spiritual renaissance in our country." This confession—which many delegates probably didn't grasp—is perhaps the first evidence that Mark Hatfield was on the threshold of a personal transformation.

Reaction to the keynote was swift and predictable, especially to Hatfield's repudiation of the bigots "who spew forth their venom of hate." This was a convention, remember, that nominated a candidate who shortly would refuse to disavow support from admittedly racist organizations of the far right. *The Denver Post* (July 14, 1964) reported the reaction in the convention hall:

> Conservative Republican delegates by the hundreds sat in angry silence Monday night as Oregon Gov. Mark Hatfield scorched the ultra-right John Birch Society....
>
> Hatfield was applauded generously after lumping Birchers with the Ku Klux Klan and Communist party—but only part of the huge throng in the Cow Palace participated, and many Republicans ... pointedly refused to join in the applause.

There were even a few boos from delegates. By the next morning hundreds of telegrams had arrived at convention headquarters—some of them supporting Hatfield but most denouncing him as a traitor to Republicanism and a Communist sympathizer. The tone of many telegrams indicated the senders were religious as well as political conservatives. This was the first time that fundamentalists had rebuked Hatfield en masse. Evangelicals, somewhat more liberal, withheld their brickbats a while longer.

Later that month (July 1964) Hatfield issued a statement denouncing the John Birch Society for actions "detrimental to the
strength and welfare of the nation." That didn't help his popularity
rating with politically conservative Christians. After brooding over
the Christian reaction to such comments, Hatfield responded
forcefully a few months later: "There's no possibility of returning to
the past. We cannot condone reactionary thinking which would
turn our country backward."[3]

Hatfield offered only lukewarm support to the ensuing Goldwater campaign. He knew the Republican Party was in trouble.
However, after President Johnson trounced Goldwater in the
November election, Hatfield played a mediating role among the
various Republican factions. He suggested such things as a national
summit meeting of Republicans, a fresh approach to the news
media, and the appointment of a "critical issues council" to develop
position papers for the party.

There are other examples, besides the keynote address, of Hatfield's political and theological evolution. Those labeling him a
"moderate" or "liberal" pointed to his consistency on such issues as
human and civil rights. As governor, Hatfield called for Republicans, as well as Christians, to "be on the side of the little people . . .
the discriminated against," to give "human rights priority over all
other rights."[4] Such commitment to human rights was not new. He
had spearheaded the fight for the public accommodations law in
Oregon in 1953.

Next Hatfield carried his civil rights banner into nationwide
forums—first the Republican National Conventions of the 1950s,
then the National Governors Conferences of the 1960s. In 1952
Hatfield was appointed to the civil rights subcommittee at the
Republican National Convention. The subcommittee, which included such noteworthies as John Foster Dulles and Christian
Herter (each later to become secretary of state), unsuccessfully
sought to strengthen a weak civil rights plank in the party platform.
Again in 1956 convention delegates approved a weak civil rights
position.

Hatfield and his compatriots had more impact, though little
more success, at the governors' conferences in Hawaii (1961),

Pennsylvania (1962), and Florida (1963). In the first two conferences, Democrats, who held substantial majorities, rebuffed attempts by liberal Republicans to adopt strong civil rights resolutions.

The Republicans' chance of success looked no better at Miami in 1963. Only 14 of 16 Republican governors attended; there were 38 Democrats (governors of the several American territories participated in the conferences). After a series of parliamentary skirmishes, crafty Republicans—led by Rockefeller and Hatfield—forced the Democratic governors to abolish the resolutions committee to avoid voting on a liberal civil rights proposal. Later the Republicans even maneuvered the Democrats into opposing a weak, "unofficial" civil rights document which the Democrats had offered as a face-saving gesture to placate their own party. For his part in orchestrating the battle, Hatfield gained national attention.

Governor Hatfield's apparent liberalism can also be seen in his view of public welfare programs. Even though he had strong misgivings about an individual's dependence on government, Hatfield supported aid for the poor and elderly. When confronted with a tax revolt by Oregon's independent-minded voters in 1963, the governor agreed to make budget cuts everywhere *but* in welfare. "I will not be a party to moving aged and infirm people out into the streets," he told the *Christian Science Monitor* (Oct. 31, 1963).

Although Hatfield continued to warn against overdependence on the state, "which coincided with the state's dependence on federal programs,"[5] he also recognized the role of the federal government:

> The federal government is not our enemy, and those who
> preach the political philosophy that we must look upon the
> federal government as a great enemy of the American people
> are being neither accurate nor objective in their evaluation.
> The federal government is, after all, all of us—it is *not* an
> alien foreign government.[6]

This recognition came from a more experienced governor, one who realized that the federal government was a partner to other levels of government. Yet Hatfield continued to push for executive reorganization in Oregon's government; part of the reason, in Hatfield's thinking, was that strong state government would check unwarranted advance of federal agencies. Federal revenue-sharing proposals, to return some tax money to state and local governments, didn't excite Hatfield. He feared that with the money would come too many federal "strings" on how it might be spent.

Despite the governor's earlier commitment to political decentralization, in January 1965 he suggested consolidating many city and county governments in Oregon to create revitalized, effective governing units. As evidence will later indicate, this proposal never got beyond the suggestion stage.

When President Johnson announced his domestic War on Poverty, Hatfield reacted enthusiastically. But it wasn't long before his enthusiasm waned. The solution to hunger at home and abroad, he decided, lay with personal involvement—not government programs.

For all his humanitarianism, though, Hatfield struck a decidedly conservative viewpoint concerning food for Communist nations. Speaking to the Rotary Club of Philadelphia on May 27, 1964, he questioned the wisdom of selling wheat to such a "ruthless enemy" as Russia:

> We place a boycott on trade with one Communist dictatorship and sell wheat to another. We sell vital materials to Poland, which ships similar goods to Cuba. . . . We do face unique problems today . . . the Communist conspiracy—ruthless, relentless and imaginative.

Hatfield also reacted in conservative fashion to Oregon's economic problems. When he entered the statehouse in 1959, the timber industry was in a slump; when timber slumps, the whole state slumps. Fearing that Oregon was in danger of becoming one of the country's most depressed areas, the governor made economic growth his top priority. He believes that his efforts succeeded:

> In eight years we had moved from that trough where we had the highest unemployment on the West Coast to the lowest,

from where we had less than the national average income per capita to where we raised our people to higher than the national average, from where we had the lowest rate of capital investment to where we had the highest rate. In eight years, every economic barometer . . . turned around. It was not very sensational, because it was piece by piece, step by step.

Despite his aggressive support of the civil rights movement, Hatfield, at first glance, faced a related issue—civil disobedience— conservatively. As governor, he was particularly distressed to see clergymen flouting laws they considered unjust: "If clergy assume the right to disobey the authority of law, they must extend the right to everyone to disobey any law they do not like."[7]

At this point in Hatfield's life, do traditional labels—liberal, conservative, moderate—accurately describe him? Just barely. His personal Christian faith was emerging as the lynchpin of all facets of his life. He was beginning to overcome conventional labels by sketching the outline of a new, *radical* Christian politics.

For example, hunger wasn't a War on Poverty problem; it was a problem of bringing about responsible Christian use of natural resources. By 1965 Hatfield even advocated trade with Communist countries. The following year he contrasted Communist strategy in the awakening Third World with "the tired diplomacy of the Yankee dollar":

The United States government promises . . . [the poor Latin American's] national government one million dollars in economic aid while the Communist guerrilla in his living room promises him food . . . [and] liberation.[8]

Even civil disobedience can be seen in another light. First, few politicians initially understood the significance of this social phenomenon. Second, what Hatfield really opposed was the use of violence. As a Christian, he saw no problem with picket lines or marches or other peaceful demonstrations to draw attention to causes in need of correction.

Without doubt the single most important element in the transformation of Hatfield's overall Christian perspective was Vietnam. In the year between the 1964 keynote address and the 1965 National Governors Conference, Hatfield had advanced from merely questioning America's involvement in Vietnam to sharply criticizing aspects of the war itself. The governor's close friends, including his longtime assistant Travis Cross, believe the change was due to Hatfield's maturing religious perspective; by 1965 his criticism was based on (Christian) moral grounds.

In July 1965, shortly before the governors' conference, Hatfield addressed the American Legion convention in Oregon. In his speech he expressed strong opposition to the continued American bombing of nonmilitary targets in Vietnam:

> I do not believe that in the ideals of both our Judeo-Christian faith and our great political idealism can we say that bombing of nonmilitary targets which could involve the deaths of noncombatant men, women and children can ever be condoned as an action of foreign policy. . . .

"Human rehabilitation" should be America's goal in Vietnam, he told the Legionnaires, and peace efforts should include a role for the United Nations.

At the 1965 governors' conference in Minneapolis, Minnesota, Vice President Hubert Humphrey sought support for the Johnson Administration's war policy. Then, after a televised report on Vietnam from Johnson himself, Gov. Carl Sanders of Georgia introduced a resolution backing the president. Hatfield and Governor Romney of Michigan sought clarification of the resolution. Though no one clarified Sanders' proposal to the satisfaction of Hatfield and Romney, impatient supporters of the president called for a voice vote. There was a chorus of ayes, then some dissent. Hatfield reports what happened:

> I shouted out my "no" very audibly. . . . As [the newsmen] crowded around, I could hear Governor Romney saying, "I voted no, too." But, apparently, few had heard him. . . . I left the table in order not to disturb the meeting any further. . . . Governor Burns of Florida had followed me out. And before I could state my reason for voting no, he stepped in front of

the microphones and . . . said, "What you have done today is a disservice to your country."[9]

Other governors echoed Burns attack. Even Governor Rockefeller, Hatfield's old liberal ally, supported the resolution.

To clarify his concern, Hatfield prepared and distributed to conferees a statement about U.S. foreign policy:

> Until a state of emergency or war is declared [by Congress] we have the right and the responsibility to differ with the President and suggest other courses of action. I cannot support the President on what he has done so far. . . .
>
> The U.S. must exhaust all avenues toward peace. We have no moral right to commit the world and especially our people to WWIII unilaterally or by the decision of a few "experts."[10]

The following day President Johnson dispatched Air Force One to fly the governors to Washington, D.C., for a briefing on Vietnam. Johnson, who announced that he was doubling the draft call and sending another 50,000 soldiers to Vietnam, reassured all the governors except Hatfield. Romney even withdrew his negative vote of the previous day. Hatfield held his ground.

Six months later, in January 1966, Hatfield announced his candidacy for the U.S. Senate. Vietnam quickly became the key issue. His opponent, U.S. Rep. Robert Duncan, a Vietnam hawk, kept the pressure on the "dovish" governor. The dramatic roll-call vote at the 1966 National Governors Conference—in which Hatfield again was the lone objector to a resolution supporting America's Vietnam policy—did Duncan no harm. Nevertheless, in November Hatfield edged Duncan by 24,000 votes.

Two terms in the governor's chair marked a period of transition, both politically and spiritually, for Hatfield. His election to the Senate placed him in a unique position in American politics—that of an unashamed evangelical Christian politician. Evaluating the enigmatic Hatfield by conventional standards was difficult enough before his crucial second term as governor. Now, more than ever, many eyes would be upon him to see what his brand of Christian politics was all about.

Radicalization Begins: Vietnam and the Draft

> Just where do our priorities lie? Is it more important to kill a Viet Cong in South Vietnam or to save the embittered poor of our own country? Is it more important to bomb South Vietnamese villages into rubble or to reconstruct our own cities of this nation? Is it therefore important to involve ourselves in a revolutionary war in Southeast Asia or to try to prevent a revolutionary war at home?[1]

WHEN RICHARD NIXON started casting about for vice-presidential running mates in 1968, Mark Hatfield came to mind. The freshman senator from Oregon would balance the ticket geographically. He never had lost an election. Despite his battle with the Republican right, his charisma would add luster to the image of the "new Nixon."

There was one problem: Vietnam. "Richard Nixon told me that Mark was going so far out on his Vietnam position that it would be difficult for delegates to choose him for the national ticket," recalls Travis Cross. "Nixon asked me to convey that message to Mark, and I did so."

Even though Hatfield didn't temper his war criticism, Nixon associates say he was among those considered at the 1968 Republican convention in Florida. A Miami newspaper—with a page one headline—predicted a Nixon-Hatfield ticket. Even evangelist Billy Graham urged Nixon to consider such a ticket. Hatfield recalls the night of decision:

> CBS had big cables up to our room, outside the door, in case the news came it was going to be me. I got a call from Billy Graham about four o'clock in the morning saying it's going to be [Spiro] Agnew. Then Herb Klein called back and said it's

59

not decided yet and he'd call back about seven. Well, Anita Bryant and her husband had invited us out to swim in the morning, so we got up and put on our swim togs. The word came to us that it was Agnew. We went down to the lobby, and it was crammed full of press—photographers, all the people. And here I was in my Bermuda shorts and swim togs.

"What about the vice-presidency?"

I said, "Has it been decided?"

Someone said, "We've just got the word it's Agnew." I said, "That's a very good choice. Thank you, gentlemen."

They said, "Are you disappointed?"

I said, "No, I'm going swimming."

In retrospect, it is fortunate Hatfield wasn't selected. He had grown angrier and angrier as the Johnson Administration intensified the U.S. commitment of men and machines to Vietnam. After the 1968 election, President Nixon largely picked up where Johnson left off. "As vice-president, I would have had to disassociate myself from the policy of the Nixon Administration," says Hatfield.

The freshman senator became convinced that the war had seriously distorted national priorities. "In God's eyes," Hatfield declared, "the life of a Viet Cong is as valuable as one of ours."[2] He found phrases like "kill ratio," "kill a Commie for Christ," and "body count" to be obscene.

As the war raged, two changes occurred in Hatfield. First, some of his early doubts about Vietnam and U.S. foreign policy turned into firm convictions. Second, he became more disillusioned with the spiritual condition of American society. He started asking penetrating questions, and he suggested that there was a Christian answer to the American malaise—brotherly love:

> Our material possessions, our wisdom, our education are all things that we must share with other people because we are all our brother's keeper. I would much rather be a keeper than a destroyer, and that to me is what America is doing today, destroying people.[3]

Early into his Senate term, Hatfield announced his own three-point plan to resolve the Indochina conflict. He suggested de-Americanizing the war, establishing an "all-Asian" peace conference, and organizing a "Southeast Asian common market." The senator crisscrossed the nation explaining his plan—and, not incidentally, criticizing policies of the Johnson Administration. Speaking before the Harvard University Young Republican Club (March 16, 1967), Hatfield stressed Vietnam's history as an essential factor in formulating policy:

> The present course of our involvement has been charted on a distorted map. The map-makers have deliberately misrepresented the twenty-year history to justify our present involvement, and they follow their twisted path with a lack of sensitivity to political realities and priorities.

Based on his own wartime experiences in Southeast Asia and his introduction in the mid-1960s to scholarly revisionism in Vietnam's history, Hatfield was convinced that the United States was fighting under faulty rationale. Nationalism, more than communism, had prompted the reunification efforts by North Vietnam's Ho Chi Minh. And nationalism had a historical inevitability that could not be denied.

In that same Harvard speech, Hatfield warned of the danger when government lied to its citizens:

> Every time that truth is distorted or denied us, we are denied a bit of our liberty. When government spokesmen misrepresent the international situation and misrepresent our national intentions, they effectively narrow alternatives to their policies. Thus is created the tyranny of the "big lie—a tyranny of no alternatives," a tyranny that does not allow Americans the liberty of choice and that does not allow us effective voice in directing our nation's course.

Such an attack didn't help Hatfield's relations with the Democratic Administration, especially when he linked Vietnam involvement to presidential arrogance as well as to congressional irresponsibility.

Hatfield wasn't the only member of Congress to object when

President Johnson declared that many were cast in the roles of advisers, but only he—the president—made decisions on such matters as war and peace. One of those seeking to curb the power of the president was Sen. J. William Fulbright, a Democrat from Arkansas. Fulbright's National Commitment Resolution of 1967—which was defeated—would have required action by Congress before American troops could be dispatched to fight in future wars.

Shortly after the Communists' successful Tet (i.e., lunar new year) assault in late January and early February of 1968, Hatfield declared that the United States had lost the war every way but militarily—and the military situation didn't look bright. The principal reason U.S. leaders continued to fight, he believed, was to "save face." He told the *Christian Science Monitor* (July 20, 1968) that such an attitude was "immoral and unconscionable."

Hatfield's moral outrage multiplied when he learned of the barbaric slaughter of more than 100 civilian Vietnamese by U.S. troops at My Lai in 1968. However, the senator asserted that such individuals as First Lt. William Calley were not alone in their guilt:

> There is a collective guilt that all of us share, for we as a nation embarked upon a foreign civil war. We, as a people, have helped create and perpetuate this situation which is compounded by the fact that our involvement in Vietnam has been and continues to be [morally and legally] wrong.[4]

Late in February 1968 Hatfield introduced his first antiwar resolution in the Senate. Coming just after the Tet offensive and North Korea's seizure of the U.S. intelligence ship *Pueblo*, many senators were in a mood to limit presidential power. Hatfield's resolution, drafted at a time when he felt President Johnson was weighing the possibility of invading North Vietnam, provided that:

> Whereas, an extension ... of the Vietnam ground war beyond the limits of South Vietnam would constitute a widening of the present conflict beyond the intended authorization of the Gulf of Tonkin Resolution; Therefore be it:
>
> RESOLVED BY THE SENATE that if the President determines ... to extend the Vietnam ground war beyond

the limits of South Vietnam, the President shall first obtain
full participation in this decision by the United States Senate
and House of Representatives.[5]

That resolution stressed the cooperative role of Congress in
determining foreign policy, not congressional usurpation of executive responsibility. Hatfield hoped that such an approach would
attract support from moderates as well as liberals. However, the
resolution gathered little support; it failed to gain Senate approval.

Even when the president announced (on March 31, 1968) his
own retirement and bombing restrictions to encourage the start of
negotiations for peace, Hatfield remained pessimistic. After two
months of talks produced little substance, the exasperated senator
lamented that "talks, however, are not the objective—peace is."[6]
Frustrated by such limited progress in negotiations, Hatfield
changed his political strategy midway through the 1968 presidential election year. Earlier Hatfield had expressed sympathy for his
old liberal ally, Gov. Nelson Rockefeller, as a presidential
candidate—and declared that he wouldn't support Nixon for president unless the hawkish candidate altered his Vietnam stand. The
Oregon senator even suggested he might vote for Sen. Eugene
McCarthy, the Democratic dove, if the Republicans didn't nomi-
nate a peace candidate!

In mid-June, however, Hatfield stunned political observers by
declaring—following a private discussion with Nixon—that he
would support Nixon. Why? Nixon hadn't given any public indica-
tion of a change of heart about Vietnam. Hatfield's political flip-flop
was particularly vexing to Rockefeller, who was seeking to unite
liberal Republicans behind his own candidacy. Hatfield explained
his sudden about-face this way:

> If we want to change the course of the war in Vietnam, it is
> obvious to me that we must fire the men who designed this
> policy. . . . Between the two leading candidates for the Re-
> publican nomination, Richard Nixon represented the great-
> est hope for resolving the war. . . . He gave me assurances
> that he saw this war not as a military threat of an international
> monolithic Communist conspiracy but rather as an out-
> growth of the misery and injustices of life in South Vietnam.

> I agreed fully with Mr. Nixon's observation that the real
> thrust must be against the social, economic and political in-
> justices that deny people their basic right to adequate food,
> living conditions and human dignity. On the basis of our con-
> versation—and the great likelihood that Mr. Humphrey
> would be the Democratic nominee—I concluded that he
> represented the greatest hope for peace.[7]

While that statement demonstrated Hatfield's considerable
gullibility—in light of Nixon's record on foreign policy and his
general philosophy—there were practical reasons for endorsing
Nixon. Apparently, Hatfield already had concluded that Nixon
would win the nomination and possibly the election. By supporting
Nixon before the party convention in August, Hatfield was deliberately moving into a position where he might wield more influence.
The senator believed he would be more effective firing from within
the prevailing political framework than he would be sniping from
without. Furthermore, Hatfield *was* tempted by the prospect of a
vice-presidential nomination.

After the convention, Nixon shrewdly selected Hatfield as one
of his "surrogate candidates" with authority to speak for the presidential nominee—especially on foreign policy. Nixon dispatched
Hatfield to the "lion's dens," the college campuses where the
Republican nominee was not popular. Hatfield realized that he was
damaging his own image by speaking on Nixon's behalf, but he felt
he had no alternative:

> And they sent me to the tough places . . . to Rutgers Univer-
> sity, to the University of Pennsylvania. They sent me to
> make the speech on behalf of Nixon and Agnew [before]
> those college crowds. And I went to those places and I stood
> there losing my credibility by the moment with those audi-
> ences, except that I went in by saying, "What are our alter-
> natives? Do you want one of the architects of the architec-
> tural firm of Vietnam, Mr. Humphrey? Do you want a racist,
> Mr. Wallace?" And usually they'd laugh and say O.K.—not
> that I persuaded them, but at least I came out with my
> credibility.

In the waning weeks of the campaign, Hatfield's doubts increased. He publicly questioned Agnew's knowledge of foreign affairs. A month before the election he authored an editorial in the *Ripon Forum* (published by the Ripon Society, an organization of liberal young Republicans) challenging political candidates to "face up to the issue of peace." The continuing talks notwithstanding, Hatfield asked the candidates to assert their views on Vietnam. "The Paris peace talks should not become the skirts for timid men to hide behind," he wrote. "There are many legitimate questions that can be put to candidates. What is their position on the bombing of North Vietnam?"

While Hatfield didn't mention Nixon's name, the senator clearly pointed out that none of the candidates had addressed the Vietnam question adequately. Many conservatives considered Nixon to be Hatfield's prime target. The editorial is evidence of Hatfield's declining confidence in the Republican candidate. After Nixon won in November, Hatfield was one of the first GOP senators to warn the new president not to ignore Vietnam. In fact, Hatfield predicted that Nixon was doomed politically unless he ended the war by 1970.

Even after Nixon was inaugurated, Hatfield continued to speak out—criticizing such policies as the incongruity of escalating the fighting with one hand while brandishing peace proposals with the other. In July 1969 the president invited Hatfield to the White House to offer a prayer of thanksgiving on behalf of America's moon-walking astronauts. The senator didn't confine his prayer to outer space:

> [Lord] excite our imagination to transfer this genius of cooperation and spirit of teamwork to our many other needs, lest our success on the moon mock our failures on the earth.
>
> Even as our astronauts go to the moon in the name of peace, our world aches from the pain of wars. We perfect the means for destroying human life and then believe we have found security. May the nations trust not in the power of their arms but in the Prince of Peace, thy Son.[8]

It was a long time before Hatfield received another invitation to the White House! Before the year was out he had voted with other

senators to repeal the Gulf of Tonkin Resolution, supported the
October 15 Vietnam moratorium sponsored by antiwar groups,
and co-sponsored (with Democratic Sen. Frank Church of Idaho) a
Senate resolution calling for the withdrawal of all troops from
Vietnam.

By the end of the 1960s Hatfield had emerged as the strongest
Republican critic on Vietnam. His record in foreign affairs was
already radical. He and other dissenting senators had been meeting for weeks to determine the proper time to launch a frontal
attack on administration policy. Even as he and Sen. George
McGovern, a South Dakota Democrat, labored to draft a major
antiwar amendment, President Nixon ordered U.S. forces to in-
vade Cambodia in early May 1970.

Hatfield and McGovern, the Senate's leading doves, quickly
completed their amendment. Shortly after the invasion began,
they tacked the "amendment to end the war" (also called the
Hatfield-McGovern amendment) to a military procurement bill.

The amendment prescribed radical action—withdrawing from
Cambodia within thirty days; ending military operations in Laos by
Dec. 30, 1970; removing U.S. troops from Vietnam by June 30,
1971, and, after Dec. 30, 1970, limiting tax monies to the safe,
systematic withdrawal of American forces.

Co-sponsors of the amendment included Republican Charles
Goodell of New York and Democrats Alan Cranston of California
and Harold Hughes of Iowa. They joined Hatfield and McGovern
in seeking to persuade both fellow senators and the American
public that such drastic legislation was the proper course. The
sponsors and their supporters purchased prime network television
time the evening of May 12, 1970, to argue their case. For his part,
Hatfield questioned the administration's Vietnamization policy,
decried the enormous cost of the war, and criticized those who
were afraid to admit error:

> . . . if it's to be humiliated to admit we're wrong and to save
> lives, then the sooner we do this, the better it's going to be
> for our nation. But I don't consider it humiliation. I consider
> it greatness, because only the powerful can take the chance
> of admitting error. . . .[9]

Shortly before the Sept. 1, 1970, vote on the amendment, Hatfield summarized his reasons for opposing Nixon's Vietnam policy:

—First, Vietnamization would not work. Said Hatfield: "Vietnamization has been defined to mean . . . we will continue to fight for the Vietnamese as long as they cannot fight on their own."[10]

—Second, despite what critics claimed, setting a precise withdrawal date for U.S. forces would have a positive effect on the Vietnam peace talks in Paris.

—Third, terms of the amendment did not mean the United States was abandoning the South Vietnamese.

—Fourth, the amendment did not infringe upon the president's war power; rather, the amendment reasserted the proper role of Congress in foreign policy.

—Fifth, the "domino theory" (which held that if one Southeast Asia nation fell to the Communists, others would follow) was simply rationalization for unending American involvement.

Just before the Senate vote, McGovern delivered an emotional plea for support of the amendment: "This chamber reeks of blood. Every senator here is partly responsible for human wreckage. There aren't many of these blasted and broken boys who think this war is a glorious venture."

The doves' arguments proved futile. The Senate rejected the Hatfield-McGovern amendment, 55 to 39. (Thirty-four Republicans and twenty-one Democrats voted against the amendment; thirty-two Democrats and seven Republicans voted for it.) Nevertheless, Hatfield and McGovern were encouraged. When they introduced the amendment, they had only a handful of supporters. At the outset, they didn't even anticipate thirty-nine votes.

A few months later, on Jan. 27, 1971, McGovern and Hatfield tried again. This time they introduced a full-fledged bill, called the Vietnam Disengagement Act of 1971. A major provision included cutting off funds for troop levels exceeding 284,000 in Southeast Asia after May 1971. In addition, after May 1, 1971, funds could be used only for releasing prisoners of war, providing asylum for Vietnamese, and for withdrawing troops—and withdrawal had to be completed by Dec. 31, 1971.

"A negotiated settlement is the means for ending the war," Hatfield declared on the Senate floor. "A timetable for withdrawal is the means to enable authentic negotiations. It is also the means for assuring the return of our prisoners of war."

Partly because of growing public concern about the prisoners of war, and partly because there was no action on the Vietnam Disengagement Act, Hatfield and McGovern changed tactics. On June 4, 1971, they introduced another end-the-war amendment, this time as a rider to a selective service bill. There were significant differences in the new amendment. The withdrawal of troops covered all Indochina, not just Vietnam. As a concession to moderates, they removed some funding restrictions and made the withdrawal date contingent upon proper response from North Vietnam concerning the release of prisoners.

In the Senate June 10, 1971, six days before the vote, Hatfield reviewed the effect of the stop-the-war amendment a year earlier:

> We were told that those who supported our amendment were not the only ones who were for peace, that all senators were for peace. . . . But what has happened since that time? Has the policy the Senate chose to follow brought us any closer to peace? Three-quarters of a year has gone by since that time. . . . 2,811 Americans have died in Indochina; 11,250 Americans have been wounded—16,578 South Vietnamese soldiers have died, and about 100,000 North Vietnamese soldiers, according to the Pentagon, have died. . . . Thousands of civilians in Indochina have been killed or wounded. And we are no closer to peace.

Despite such rhetoric, and the concessions in the amendment, the doves gained little the second time around. The Senate defeated the second Hatfield-McGovern amendment 55 to 42—a gain of just three "yes" votes.

Hatfield's purposes in sponsoring end-the-war amendments included a Christian concern for human lives as well as political and constitutional reasons. The senator believed there was no constitutional justification for President Nixon's war policy, particularly after the Senate repealed the Gulf of Tonkin Resolution in 1973. As

Hatfield became more radical in his understanding of the positive role of Congress, he became increasingly distressed at how the legislative branch had relinquished responsibility to the president:

> We cannot avoid the harsh reality that we, the elected members of this body, share in the responsibility for those who are wounded and who die in this war. That is what our Constitution intends. We cannot pretend that we can abdicate this responsibility—that we can call on the president to bear that heaviest of all burdens. [11]

Hatfield also opposed the war because it was fought largely by draftees. He believed military conscription to be alien to American democratic principles. His Senate seat was scarcely warm when he introduced his first antidraft bill in March 1967. That bill, the Armed Forces Improvements Act of 1967, sought to end the draft and improve the quality of a future all-volunteer military. In Hatfield's eyes, conscription was a "pernicious . . . invasion of the individual liberty that eight generations of Americans had fought to preserve. Personal liberty is not a privilege. It is not a concession granted by government that must be paid for by military service. It is the guaranteed right of democracy. It must not be compromised."[12]

Hatfield also opposed the draft because it was inequitable. "We cannot tolerate the injustice of a system that capriciously requisitions two years out of the lives of some men while allowing others their liberty," he told fellow senators. In addition, he warned that the draft provided quantity rather than quality, cranking out ill-trained, short-term soldiers when the nation needed career troops thoroughly familiar with sophisticated weapons. The draft lottery—an alternative advanced by some congressmen—wasn't satisfactory either.

"The lottery is a patchwork proposal to cover some of the gaping holes in the fabric of military conscription," Hatfield declared in the Senate, "but it does little to retailor the flaws in the basic design of the draft." Specifically, he thought the lottery unfair because it forced some to serve two years while others didn't serve at all. And the lottery, like the basic draft, remained inefficient and costly.

That initial antidraft bill received just moderate support. Two years later, in January 1969, he introduced a similar bill. This time his co-sponsors included Senators McGovern, Robert Dole, a Republican from Kansas, and—surprisingly—Barry Goldwater. (Though Hatfield, the dove, and Goldwater, the hawk, remained far apart on such matters as Vietnam, they saw eye to eye on the need for a professional army.) One additional provision to the bill accelerated the substitution of civilian for military personnel in noncombat positions.

Again the antidraft measure was unsuccessful. Hatfield tried once more, in 1970. By this time critics of the volunteer army argued that it soon would be composed of only blacks and the poor. That argument, Hatfield suggested, was an insult. "[It] questions the poor and the blacks' capacity to make decisions in their own best interest."

The other major complaint was that a volunteer army would be a collection of presumably disloyal mercenaries. To that, Hatfield replied in Senate debate: "To question the loyalty of a soldier because he is paid a fair salary is like questioning the loyalty of doctors. . . ." Once again, the odd-couple combination of Hatfield and Goldwater was unable to carry the Senate; the volunteer-army bill was defeated. Later, of course, a similar measure was approved—but it was not a Hatfield bill.

While the stop-the-war and end-the-draft measures failed, the two issues combined to give Hatfield high visibility throughout the late 1960s and early 1970s. But while his popularity blossomed among political progressives throughout the country, evangelicals were not so pleased with the senator from Salem.

The Trouble With Senator Hatfield

> Dear Senator Hatfield: I want to make it clear that when I did vote for you, I did not cast that vote with the idea of making you more powerful than the President. (What higher power is there than President Nixon?) . . . Have you forgotten that God's way is to respect and honor those in authority?
>
> Letter to Mark Hatfield[1]

> The Bible [Hatfield responds] gives us no basis for uncritically accepting the state, or rejecting it either. Rather, the Bible tells us that at times, Caesar and God may come into conflict. Of course, we know what our priority is.[2]

ANGRY AMERICANS jammed Senator Hatfield's mailbox with letters protesting his antiwar beliefs. The most vicious of the letters came from fellow Christians, several of them accusing the senator of making himself "more powerful than the president." One, who identified himself as a Christian, suggested "shooting rioters that throw rocks"—and he accused Hatfield of treason.

One day Hatfield stepped out of his private office and noticed a young secretary sobbing softly. Concerned, he quietly inquired what was wrong. She shook her head and tried to hide the letter on her desk. The senator, sensing the problem, asked to see the letter. Reluctantly, she showed it to him.

After scanning the letter—which was from a particularly sharp-tongued Christian—Hatfield admonished his secretaries to show him even the worst mail. "I've got to see them," he said. "You can't hide them from me."

To be sure, Hatfield didn't shrink from opportunities to speak to conservative evangelicals, even when he knew his message would

71

infuriate many of them. One of his first such occasions was June 1967, when he addressed the Southern Baptist Convention:

> God does not intend that human beings should suffer endlessly under pressures of poverty, hunger, social decay, racial persecution, disease, ignorance, unemployment, war, or violence.
>
> . . . we have an obligation to use our creative genius to find alternatives to war, alternatives that will not consign our youth, our greatest national resource, to an endless conflict. [3]

Despite Hatfield's call to pursue peace rather than war, the convention spurned his advice and approved a pro-war resolution.

Evangelical opposition to the senator peaked after his September 1969 speech, titled "The Path to Peace," before the United States Congress on Evangelism in Minneapolis, Minnesota. He criticized evangelicals for their lack of compassion for the needs of people and for not being peacemakers:

> I reject the simplistic notion that peace is the absence of conflict. Peace is not merely stability or order. Rather, peace is fulfillment, harmony, satisfaction, understanding, and well-being.
>
> As long as there is deprivation, suffering, alienation, self-seeking, exploitation, there is no real peace. . . .
>
> It is my conviction that peace will not come to Vietnam as long as we persist in applying military solutions to fundamentally social, political and cultural problems.
>
> We intervened in what was essentially a civil war, in my judgment, having its origins in the desire of the Vietnamese people to rid their country of foreign domination and bring themselves independence and dignity. This cause has been constantly frustrated . . . and now even by our own involvement. . . . By interpreting the war as an ideological struggle, we have lost sight of the human dimension of the conflict—of the passion, will, and suffering of individuals which lie at the roots of this war. . . .
>
> Why should we—a nation founded by those seeking a New World blessed by God—now be bound by "an eye for an eye, a tooth for a tooth"? Do the fruits of the Spirit—love,

joy, peace, patience, kindness, generosity . . . and self-control—do these have any relevance to the concrete realities we face?[4]

Within a few months Hatfield's indictment was reprinted in several Christian magazines. They were difficult words for those conservative evangelicals who already were convinced that America's cause in Vietnam was righteous. In their eyes, Hatfield heaped on more burning coals a few months later when he and Senator McGovern introduced their first end-the-war amendment. Letter writers chastised Hatfield for his views. One, who identified himself as a "former brother in Christ"—with the clear implication that Hatfield was the "brother" whose position had changed—addressed the senator with a mild obscenity:

> Dear: I heard you speak at the Men's Fellowship at my church a year ago and at that time you believed in Jesus Christ as your personal Lord and Savior. Now because you won't support the boys in Vietnam and you're fighting President Nixon who has been placed there by God, I know that you're not.[5]

There were many others:

> A member of your Oregon staff talked to me recently and pointed out your strong religious feelings. I doubt this very much because you are against the military which guarantees religious freedom and democracy for this nation.[6]
>
> I and a lot of other Christian people are extremely disappointed in your performance in the Senate, for you who claim to be a Christian and have access to our Almighty God should have a better understanding of human nature and evil in the human heart.[7]
>
> The trouble with Senator Hatfield . . . is that he has confused his own philosophy with the true teachings of Jesus.
>
> There is a fundamental difference between killing for murder and acting as an agent of God's processes. How else does He work His will? All talk of ending the Indochina war . . . before the Communists are stopped is immoral . . . and even irreligious.[8]

That wasn't all. In December 1969 Hatfield delivered a reading of "The Incomparable Christ" on evangelist Oral Roberts' Christmas telecast. The telecast was recorded. Later Hatfield received mail containing the record—smashed into pieces.

In 1970, as he had the previous dozen years, Hatfield attended the Oregon Conservative Baptists' fall Men's Round-Up to teach the Sunday school lesson. Rumors circulated that some of the 1,249 men would leave when Hatfield was introduced. The walkout didn't materialize; just one person left, and the men gave the senator a standing ovation at the close of the lesson—which was about Christian fellowship. Even so, the presence of such rumors, along with the hate mail and other incidents, upset Hatfield.

> I was shocked, dismayed, depressed. Down inside of me my feelings began to eat away in a manner I could barely control. Part of me wanted to lash back. To this day I cannot understand how believing Christians who had given their allegiance to the Prince of Peace could cheer on the nation in that despicable and inhumane War. . . .
>
> What am I doing all this for anyway? I asked myself. What's the purpose of coming back to Washington . . . splitting up time between the demands of being a husband to my wife and father to my four children? . . . Going out and giving stirring speeches about the immorality of the War, I would sense a tremendous responsiveness; but then, I'd go home, and the audience would go home, and the War would go on. . . . There was merit in raising crucial issues, but the battles were never won. . . .[9]

Those were crisis days for Hatfield. "He was tremendously hurt that those who profess Christ could have an antagonistic feeling," recalls Douglas Coe. "It is just like when your wife says something that hurts you: You can appreciate their problem or position technically, but if it comes with a certain venom from someone that you love or care about, you don't expect it. It is the venom that hurts."

Hatfield was so frustrated that he seriously considered resigning from the Senate. "If I have to pay this price to stay in politics, to go through estrangement from my brothers, I'm not sure this is a price I'm willing to pay," he said.[10] In retrospect, he recalls that time of great questioning.

Am I where I should be in terms of God's will? And I had all sorts of reasons to think maybe I wasn't, that I might be closer to God's will by removing myself from that center stage and seeking some other pursuit.

What drove some of my friends and supporters up the wall was that I would make no commitment. They kept saying, "You have to make a decision to run or not to run. You can't stay in limbo. You've got a lot of political rebuilding to do if you want to run for a second term. If you don't, fine—hang it up."

And I didn't know, I really didn't. If anything at that point, I figured I would hang it up.

At the peak of Hatfield's personal crisis, he traveled to Pasadena, California, to speak at Fuller Theological Seminary's commencement exercises (June 2, 1970). The senator was aware that some wealthy supporters of the seminary hadn't been pleased with the choice of speakers. Yet, he wasn't willing to temper his talk for the benefit of the conservatives in the audience:

> So I went there with great fear and trepidation. I've never been so scared. I was met by Dave Hubbard [the president of Fuller] and we walked over to the First Methodist Church where the commencement was held. . . . Dave said, "Mark, I want you to come in and just say a word to the graduating class before we start the commencement." We walked back to this room and fully one-third of the graduating class had black bands on their gowns in protest of the war. I walked in and they started cheering. Well, I just was overcome emotionally. . . . We walked to the platform and I turned to face the audience. In the back, a homemade wrapping paper sign was being unrolled across the full length of that balcony. It said, "We're with you, Mark." . . . I was so choked up that if it hadn't been for the hymn and prayers . . . I'm not sure I could have done anything except stand there and blubber. . . .
>
> Well, when I got home I told Dave Hubbard, "You know, it had to be God at work. It proves so much about my little faith." That was also a great blow to me that I had fretted and fumed and said, "I'm committing it to you," but I really hadn't.[11]

That experience was a spiritual turning point for Hatfield. "It demonstrated to me that there were countless evangelicals, who because of their faith in Christ, could not condone the immoral and barbarian violence our nation was inflicting throughout Indochina," he said.[12]

Another hopeful event during those difficult times was the appearance of a new evangelical publication called *Post American*. "Here was a group of committed evangelicals who were articulating the imperatives of the Gospel for our time and our society in a compelling and biblical fashion," the senator wrote.[13] The response at Fuller and encounters with those who published *Post American* convinced Hatfield that there still was hope for evangelicals.

Thus revitalized, the senator went home to Oregon in the fall of 1971. During a weekend at the beach with his wife, he cast aside thoughts of resigning his Senate seat and decided to seek re-election in 1972. But no longer was he concerned with the results of the election. He had decided that if God wanted him in politics, fine. If not, he would find another way to serve God. Said Hatfield: "I began to feel liberated from the idolatry of power and given over more deeply to a whole new vision of prophetic witness, faithfulness, and servanthood."[14]

Although Hatfield wasn't worried about reelection, his constituents were concerned. Some felt he was so busy with Vietnam that he was ignoring Oregon. The state Republican hierarchy didn't appreciate Hatfield's strident criticism of President Nixon. Mark Enna, chairman of the Oregon Republican Party, noted that "if Senator Hatfield's views are so out of step with the Nixon Administration, he would better serve the two-party system by changing his registration."[15]

A mid-1971 political poll forecast plenty of problems for Hatfield. It indicated that Republican Gov. Tom McCall, who was weighing a primary challenge for the Senate seat, would whip Hatfield without breaking a sweat. And even if Hatfield could avoid a primary fight, the same poll showed that U.S. Rep. Edith Green, a Democrat, would defeat him in the general election if she chose to move to the Senate.

The predictions of doom proved incorrect. In mid-August McCall decided to finish his second term in the statehouse rather than challenge Hatfield. The Nixon Administration made no attempt to "purge" Hatfield—as the White House had done with New York's Senator Goodell in 1970, in retaliation for his opposition to the war. And Hatfield's general-election opponent turned out to be Wayne Morse, the former senator who earlier had applauded Hatfield's Vietnam criticism.

With the liberal Morse in the race, Oregon's largest daily newspapers—the *Oregonian* and *Oregon Journal* in Portland—editorially backed Hatfield. There was no formal opposition from conservative Christians. Morse's age (72) was a handicap. Even though Nixon easily defeated Senator McGovern—Hatfield's stop-the-war compatriot—in Oregon's presidential voting, the senator had little trouble whipping Morse.

Although the campaign turned out to be relatively dull, that victory marked another personal milestone for Hatfield. In 1966 he had triumphed over political ambition. Now, in 1972, he was convinced that God wanted him in politics—and that he was not alone. Through his Fuller Seminary speech and his contact with the *Post American*, he had discovered a substantial community of young evangelicals who shared his desire to integrate faith and politics.

Hatfield began to question "the system" even more substantially. As governor he had shown little sympathy for those seeking change via open dissent. As a senator, though, his perspective changed. In 1971 he even considered withholding payment of his income taxes as a protest against the Vietnam conflict. He sympathized with the war dissenters and was truly incensed by the tactics of the Johnson and Nixon Administrations against "unpatriotic" demonstrators. He claimed that both presidents failed to realize that

> the freedom to stand opposed to the government's policy, the freedom to speak out against government actions which corrupt the basic tenets of our society, that this freedom is not a privilege which can be withdrawn when the boat begins to rock.

This freedom is the inherent and ultimate right of a people in a democracy. It is a right that supersedes any ambitions or complexes of men and stands above the gravity of any issue. . . .

When you start to impugn the patriotism of a critic, you are, in effect, not trying to persuade but to destroy your critics.[16]

Patriotism has to be based on convictions, faithfulness to American ideals and credibility of national leaders. But it should not require Americans to line up shoulder to shoulder, and in the name of blind faith and national unity, endorse bad policy.[17]

Hatfield rejected the law-and-order mentality of political conservatives. Riots, he said, could be controlled not by laws but by dealing with the causes—poverty, hunger, and racism. In his mind, there was a direct link between urban unrest among minorities and the fact that the minorities suffered the heaviest burdens of the Vietnam War. Only love could heal the rift caused by the war—and by a government which demanded too much loyalty from its citizens. He wondered whether the unresponsive system was open to change at all.

I've worked within the system all my life, and I believe in our system. But when I look at what we need to do, and I see how much time it takes, how hard you have to shove to get the slightest response, I have to agree some days with the kids who say it may not be enough. It may not be enough. . . .[18]

He also believed that the greatest danger to our democracy came not from without but from

unresponsive, archaic machinery of government; from estranged, disenfranchised citizens who insist that the "system" does not work; from racial strife and antagonism; and from deteriorating cities and their embittered, impoverished citizens.[19]

Despite his seeming disenchantment with an unresponsive government, Hatfield wasn't ready to give up totally on the American brand of democracy. Writing in the *Oregonian's Northwest Maga-*

zine (July 25, 1971), he indicated that, although painfully slow, our system does occasionally respond:

> Although I can understand the frustration and disillusionment with government held by many of our citizens, and feel it myself at times, I do not believe the pessimists are justified in giving up and saying that it is no longer possible to work through the system. Rather I believe there are instances when the system has worked. . . .
>
> [One example] was in 1968, when the force of public opinion drove Lyndon Johnson out of the White House. There is no question in my mind that Lyndon Johnson fled the White House because of political fright. . . .
>
> The salvation of our political institutions depends upon their willingness to reform themselves. . . . Faith in our system will be preserved only if it keeps pace with the changes sweeping our country. That can happen only when its citizens act on that faith. . . .

What then of civil disobedience for Christians? Hatfield was convinced that the Christian's ultimate loyalty is to God, not to human government. While not advocating wholesale disregard of man's regulations, he pointed out that a blanket rejection of civil disobedience for Christians would imply that the laws of the state and God's plan always harmonize. This ran counter to his vision of the nature of the state as taught in the New Testament. His perspective was moving him far beyond the place where obedience to the state could be proclaimed unconditionally.

A Prophetic Christian Politics

There is a theological "silent majority" in our land who wrap
their Bibles in the American flag, who believe that conservative politics is the necessary by-product of orthodox Christianity, who equate patriotism with the belief in national
self-righteousness, and who regard political dissent as a
mark of infidelity to the faith.[1]

The notion that being evangelical means that one does not
have to concern himself with social problems, or that ministering to social ills is different from an evangelical concern, is
simply heretical, whichever way you look at it.[2]

NOT UNTIL HE slipped into his chair at the head table did
Senator Hatfield feel the tension. President Nixon sat at his right,
Billy Graham at his left. The National Prayer Breakfast audience
was a prestigious throng, numbering more than 3,000 cabinet
officers, influential congressmen, Supreme Court justices, uni-
formed military officers, foreign diplomats, and the upper echelon
of industry and education.

A few days earlier Sen. John Stennis, a Democrat from Mississippi, had asked Hatfield to speak briefly at the annual breakfast—
to provide political "balance." (The previous year conservative
Sen. Strom Thurmond of South Carolina had represented the
Senate.)

Reluctantly Hatfield accepted the invitation from Stennis, an
evangelical. He had two major concerns: First, he didn't want to
mix "piety and patriotism" and thus somehow convey Divine
sanction upon the works of men through such events as prayer
breakfasts. Second, he was unsure of the "message" he should
deliver.

81

Hatfield sought advice from Douglas Coe, director of "The Fellowship"—the organization which sponsored the prayer breakfast—and from Jim Wallis, editor of the radical Christian magazine *Post American* (now named *Sojourners*). Both Coe and Wallis urged Hatfield to speak forthrightly as prompted by the Holy Spirit, not to tone down criticism of government and the war. The senator followed their advice. There was much on his mind, for the Nixon Administration was then pointing with pride to the "peace with honor" just achieved in Vietnam. And just seven months earlier, a presidential spokesman had dismissed the invasion of Democratic National Committee offices in the Watergate complex as an act by "third-rate burglars."

As Hatfield rose to speak, he remembers "looking out into the audience and seeing frowning, hostile looks on the faces of [top White House aides] Bob Haldeman and John Ehrlichman, seated directly in front."[3] Calmly the senator dropped this bomb in the laps of assembled VIPs:

> If we leaders appeal to the god of civil religion, our faith is in a small and exclusive deity, a loyal spiritual advisor to power and prestige, a Defender of only the American nation, the object of a national folk religion devoid of moral content. But if we pray to the biblical God of justice and righteousness, we fall under God's judgment for calling upon His name, but failing to obey His command. . . .
>
> We sit here today, as the wealthy and the powerful. But let us not forget that those who follow Christ will more often find themselves not with comfortable majorities, but with miserable minorities.
>
> Today, our prayers must begin with repentance. Individually, we must seek forgiveness for the exile of love from our hearts. And corporately as a people, we must turn in repentance from the sin that scarred our national soul. . . .
>
> We need a "confessing church"—a body of people who confess Jesus as Lord and are prepared to live by their confession. Lives lived under the Lordship of Jesus Christ at this point in our history may well put us at odds with the values of our society, abuses of political power, and cultural

conformity of our church. . . . Let us be Christ's messengers
of reconciliation and peace, giving our lives over to the
power of His love. Then we can soothe the wounds of war,
and renew the face of the earth and all mankind.[4]

The audience, momentarily stunned, finally responded with
sustained, energetic applause. But during that embarrassing, quiet
interim, *Newsweek* observed that "no one in the audience was
heard to say, 'Amen.'"[5] Wesley Pippert, a reporter for United
Press International, concluded that Hatfield turned the prayer
breakfast into "one of the most dramatic confrontations since the
Prophet Nathan told King David, 'You are the man!'"[6]

Hatfield says he didn't intend his comments to be a personal
attack on the president—but that is how many listeners apparently
reacted. The senator was dismayed to discover that White House
officials were "infuriated" by his presentation. (Later in 1973 Hatfield learned that his name was among those on the lengthy White
House "enemies list.") The next day's *New York Times* carried a
22-paragraph story about the breakfast, devoting just two paragraphs to the president's remarks and twelve paragraphs to Hatfield and his talk:

> President Nixon, the Rev. Billy Graham and three Russian
> atheists were among the more than 3,000 people who at-
> tended the 21st National Prayer Breakfast . . . and heard a
> long-time foe of the Vietnam war call it "a sin that has scarred
> the national soul."
>
> With the President and his wife sitting inches away,
> Senator Mark O. Hatfield . . . told the audience of Govern-
> ment leaders and their friends and families that they should
> seek individual and collective forgiveness for the country's
> role in the hostilities there.[7]

There was a remarkable public response to the prayer breakfast
confrontation. Much of the senator's mail was supportive. Christian periodicals throughout the country sought permission to print
Hatfield's speech. Some "establishment evangelicals," though,
succumbed to the lure of civil religion and condemned the speech
outright; others, including Billy Graham, reacted ambivalently. In

a letter to Hatfield shortly after the breakfast, Graham praised the senator for boldly proclaiming the name of Christ and suggested that some civil religion practices at such functions had departed from the original Prayer Breakfast format. On the other hand, the evangelist noted with "deep concern" that the press had inter- preted Hatfield's remarks as a personal rebuke to President Nixon. Graham went on to say:

> It seems to me that the Breakfast should be a time of praying for and encouraging our political leaders—especially the President!
>
> If I had any suggestion to make it would have been that you as a war critic could have turned to the President and commended him for his determination and perseverance in getting the cease-fire in Vietnam. . . .
>
> As you already know I have an affection for President Nixon as a man and as a personal friend. I believe him to be one of the most sincere, dedicated and able men ever to occupy The White House. He has shaken history as no other President since Roosevelt. He has set an example in self- discipline, family life, church attendance, et cetera, that is helping the Country through a great spiritual crisis—and despite differences in certain political areas he deserves to be commended especially by Christians.[8]

During Hatfield's early years in the Senate, such issues as civil religion, Vietnam, the draft, and evangelical hostility combined to play an important role in the transformation of his Christian world view. That transformation also resulted from many theological and cultural forces, including Hoover Republicanism, mainline evangelicalism, the senator's Baptist heritage, and, to some extent, Reformed Christianity. The dominant force, however, seems to have been, and continues to be, "radical Anabaptism."

Radical Anabaptism can best be interpreted as a contemporary, revitalized expression of the theology of historic Anabaptism (which means, literally, "to baptize again"). Such Anabaptist thought is found, for example, among the free-church movements, Mennonites, Brethren, and, to some extent, Quakers. From these natural sources, radical Anabaptists inherit concern for themes like the sanctity of human life, communal Christianity, and suspicion of government and politics. To this legacy, radical Anabaptists, who are found in historic Anabaptist circles and in blossoming "communities" across America, add unique local touches.

Today, radical Anabaptists focus on the implications of phrases like "revolutionary subordination," the "power of servanthood," "countercultural Christianity," "prophetic politics," and standing "over-against" exploiters while siding with the poor and the oppressed.[9] Radical Anabaptists prophetically speak out against war and nuclear weapons, human poverty, and governmental arrogance. They take strong stands for world peace based on love, an equitable sharing of the earth's resources, and self-government based on individuals and small communities.

It is small wonder that Hatfield should gravitate toward radical Anabaptism. Any evangelical reacting against perceived cancers of American society, and being persecuted for such views, would find the radical Anabaptist perspective appealing. It is a substantial world view with a solid theological foundation. (Yet we will see that substantive questions can be directed at those who share this world view.)

Completing the remarkable transition from typical evangelicalism to radical Anabaptism didn't mean that Hatfield abandoned all evangelical presuppositions. He remained faithful to the basic evangelical understanding of Scripture, Christ, the sovereignty of God, and the centrality of the love commandment in the life of the Christian. He also struggled to maintain a balance between theological individualism and concern for the community.

One emphasis, however, really distinguished Hatfield from mainstream evangelicals during the late 1960s—his thorough condemnation of the failures of the institutional church. Because of his growing understanding of the unity of life provided by Christianity, he was unable to accept the typical dualism of conservative evangelicals who used theology to justify a convenient separation from the problems of the world. Instead, Hatfield called for a Christian "infiltration" into the world to identify with human suffering wherever it was found. In effect, he sought a separation "in the mode of our living, in attitudes, manners, words, deeds; our life is distinctive. It is unique, separate from the mundane of the world, but we are not isolated from the world."[10]

Dualism limited the church's sensitivity to the total needs of mankind—physical as well as spiritual. "If our only motivation is to get [the individual] 'saved,' I don't think we are being scriptural,"[11] he asserted in 1968. Those concentrating on soul-saving had distorted the scriptural message of self-giving love and identification with those in need:

> Have you [Christians] been down to a rescue mission on skid row? How easy it is to love the lovely. But try loving someone who has vomit all over the front of his clothes. A dirty, stinking creature of God. That is the test of how real our love of mankind is. How strong is our love for those of different colored skins? Of different economic classes?[12]

Hatfield was especially critical of the church's failure to follow Christ's example of identifying with the needy. By its noninvolvement, the senator said, the church has "painted Jesus Christ as a respectable, suburban, stand-pat establishmentarian, defending the status quo, instead of recognizing Him as the greatest political, social, economic, and spiritual revolutionary the world has ever known."[13] Hatfield reminded evangelicals that Christ himself had

> minced no words in rebuking those who loved to sit in the front seats at church and who said their prayers loudly in public as demonstrations of their righteousness. Christ warned that such outward pretension only further demonstrated the necessity for inner repentance. He looked for practice rather than pious rhetoric. Much of our religious establishment today needs to hear again the whole truth of Christ's message. With the serious issues of war, race, hunger, and poverty impinging upon us, the Christian must follow Christ in deeds as well as words.[14]

By the late 1960s, Hatfield's opinion of dualistic evangelicals had reached a new low: "The poor will always fade into the background while the pious go to church."[15] Because of sentiments such as these, his support from conservative evangelicals dissolved rapidly.

Senator Hatfield was able to transcend most vestiges of conservatism during the late 1960s. He abandoned much of his earlier political focus on limited moral issues, concentrating instead on the regrettable moral "vacuum" which occurred when Christians withdrew from public life, especially politics. He also realized that the solution to immorality in public office rested on the ethical character of the American people themselves. One exception to his flight from the confines of political moralism was his concern about pornography in America, but even on this issue he cautioned against using the government to enforce prohibition. Instead he sought firm and reasonable legal guidelines to protect citizens, especially the young, from exploitation.

One of the best examples of Hatfield's transcendence of theological conservatism is the issue of civil religion. He opposed the identification of evangelical theology with political extremism: "And God, to the far righters, is a personification of a white, Protestant, anti-Communist American. They have turned the scriptural tables and created God in their image."[16] Right-wingers, he declared, were not practicing true biblical fundamentalism; rather, they had turned love of country into an "idol," thereby violating the first commandment. (Idolatry was not limited to the political right, for Hatfield also warned against absolutizing from the political left.)

Because of his fear of extremism, Hatfield was unnerved by attempts to speak of "Christian" positions on specific issues. Extremists from the right preached that there could be just one true Christian position—theirs! In rejecting that simplistic approach, Hatfield hesitated to acknowledge that Christians could develop political answers sufficiently faithful to Scripture to be uniquely "Christian" (and thus applicable to all believers). "I think it is a mistake to be so dogmatic that we think that there is a . . . Christian position," he said, "and that therefore every other position must be either anti-Christian or non-Christian. . . ."[17]

Hatfield's reluctance to claim *the* Christian answer also was the product of a remnant of dualism in his own thought. He still divided his life into the realms of theology (where absolute certainty was possible) and politics (where relativity reigned supreme). This dualism did not deal so much with practical life, where Hatfield strove to fuse Christianity and politics, as with his openness to the theoretical framework of historic Anabaptism. Because of that dualism and his distrust of extremists, Hatfield had difficulty in strongly recommending his radical political proposals to other Christians for fear of also being accused of extremism.

In 1969 and 1970 Hatfield revealed many fascinating dimensions of his radical Anabaptism in three speeches to Christian audiences. Two of the speeches, "The Path to Peace" and the Fuller commencement address, have been mentioned in another context. The third, "The (Holy?) Spirit of '76" was delivered in October 1969 at John Brown University. Significantly, these addresses not only reflected Hatfield's antiwar stance and growing self-image as a "peacemaker," they also indicated his emerging prophetic role among evangelicals. As a prophet, he sought to awaken evangelicals to the fullness of the Gospel. These speeches mark his first substantial effort to spell out some radical implications of his Christian world view.

Five important themes bind the three speeches together. First, he stressed the sovereignty of God over history and the "revolutionary" significance of Christ's death and resurrection, implying that Christians should be unafraid of radical change. Christians, in fact, should be at the vanguard of change—influencing revolutions by their desire to achieve human dignity and freedom.

Second, the Gospel was revolutionary because it didn't split faith and life:

> We must not make the mistake of believing that the Good News we proclaim has no relevance to our attitudes and actions toward political ... problems ... in our ... nation, and our world.[18]

Third, since evangelicals lacked social and political direction, Hatfield noted that they were pulled toward right or left-wing ideology—what he termed the "Biblical Nationalist" and "Political Messiah" options. Both were examples of civil religion and should be avoided. He was especially sensitive to the idolatry of the presidency among conservative evangelicals. And he was beginning to emphasize the concept of corporate (i.e., national) sin, as well as the need for true Christian community.

Fourth, Hatfield countered right-wing arguments about the sanctity of the status quo by pointing out the "true" role of religion in American history. He drove a wedge between colonial and post-Revolutionary history, explaining that the former had been "religious" and the latter largely "secular."

> As the colonies met with political and economic success, the religious base of society gradually weakened. . . . they began to seek their success in so-called laws of economics and government. Thus, the success of an individualistic and capitalist economy began to be worshipped as a thing in itself rather than as an expression of the biblical concept that as a man works, so shall he prosper.
>
> Likewise, in the area of political theory, the concept of limited government—originally based on a biblically derived distrust of power under cognizance that all men were fallen creatures subject to greed and lust—became absolutized at the expense of those who had no hope but to turn to government for their protection against concentrated power of modern economic organization.
>
> Thus, while the religious basis of American society originally served as the cultural dynamic which helped assure its success, in later years it was perverted and used as a rationalization for the self-interests of those who were comfortable under the existing situation.[19]

According to Hatfield, those who are comfortable under a system of "corporate capitalism" have little sympathy for the critical problem of unequal distribution of wealth. He suggested a more radical approach:

> Let us [evangelicals] commit ourselves to the goal of seeing that each person in this nation is granted the minimal resource for well-being which is justly his by virtue of his humanity. Let us not hide from our duty by decrying socialism—creeping or otherwise—protesting the welfare state, or painting pictures of big government as a type of anti-Christ. The evangelical conscience takes its authority

not from John Locke's concept of prosperity or William
Buckley's concepts of strictly limited government, but from
the New Testament.[20]

Finally, since Hatfield believed that evangelicals are called to
identify with the poor—not with economic or political
establishments—he urged them to demonstrate the validity and
power of Christ's life in an age desperate for such a hope. He
pleaded for unified evangelical action:

> ... I believe the evangelical community has as its most
> urgent task the *developing of a responsible social and politi-
> cal ethic* that takes with equal seriousness the truth of
> Christ's life and God's revelation of himself to man and the
> crisis confronting the social and political institutions of our
> age.[21]

If the church did not move in this direction, Hatfield believed it
was in danger of losing out to the forces of secularism which had
plagued America since the Revolution. He feared secularism as
much as he did evangelical political extremism. "I believe that the
church must open its eyes to the vision of a better society, or else it
will by default share in the guilt for the nightmare of secular
ideological totalitarianism."[22]

To avoid this kind of tyranny Hatfield has resolved to (1) speak
against dualism and civil religion among evangelicals, (2) call for
national repentance due to "corporate sin," and (3) attempt to
develop societal models—political and economic—which evangelicals and others might find more equitable than our present system.

Early in the 1970s Hatfield reached the melancholy conclusion
that the Protestant church in general, and evangelicals in particular, were in a feckless condition. That is why he spoke out so
courageously at the National Prayer Breakfast in 1973 and at
Princeton Seminary's commencement in 1974. At Princeton he
called for "a new theology of Christian living," recognizing both the
"pastoral" and "prophetic" dimensions. Hatfield defined pastors as
those concerned chiefly about personal salvation and prophets as
those concerned chiefly with seeing God's purposes for the world

being realized. We need "pastor-prophets," he said, leaders who recognize that concern for the individual must be balanced by social consciousness and a desire for social justice. The senator emphasized that the prophetic dimension potentially enabled all believers, but especially evangelicals, to speak "to the spiritual depth of our nation."[23]

Because of such insight, Hatfield became the champion of the progressive neo-evangelicals plus a growing number of evangelical moderates who were searching for a relevant social and political ethic. In the months that followed, the lines of Hatfield's radical Anabaptist direction became more distinct. He sharpened his focus on such themes as a new patriotism, radical social and political involvement by evangelicals, corporate sin, community, power, leadership, compassion and pacifism, and a greater expression of love in the lives of individual Christians.

In 1973 and 1974 three of Hatfield's most radical essays were published (two in *Post American*, one in *Eternity*), reflecting in particular his growing crusade against civil religion. He wrote them in an almost desperate attempt to rescue the church from thoughtless conformity to the status quo:

> The more I observe contemporary America, . . . the more I sense how dangerous it is to merge piety and patriotism.
>
> Our politics must never be ruled by thoughtless conformity to the culture, because it is clear that our culture is not Christian in the truest sense of the word.
>
> Yet, our culture is "religious." . . . Most Americans . . . have a great faith in [a] civil religion, a religion that is nothing more than unitarianism. It includes the belief that God has blessed and chosen America as He did Israel, ... and that the Constitution and Declaration of Independence (whose authors were mostly Deists!) were written after inspired prayer meetings.
>
> But our civil religion distorts the relationship between the state and our faith. It tends to enshrine our law and order and national righteousness while failing to speak of repentance, salvation, and God's standard of justice. . . . America's actions become spiritually ordained, and even in war, we are beyond reproach. . . .

> Much of the organized church today has allowed its think-
> ing and values to be shaped by the world. It is, in many ways,
> the captive of our culture, and the religion of America is
> America.[24]

For Hatfield, materialism, poverty, and the psychology of war
were all examples of corporate sin, and they were all strengthened
by our own peculiar expression of faith in "the American way."
Because of its conformity to the American way, Hatfield considered the church as guilty of these corporate sins as the nation—
and just as subject to judgment. In his view, corporate or national
repentance was necessary but impossible, because we as a people
were unaware of all but individual sins.

The senator's awareness of corporate sin and national repentance
spawned new ideas of community, a theme emerging more clearly
since 1974 to balance his traditional theological individualism.

> We are creatures who find our identity in groups. . . . In
> man's most profound moments he has sensed his own indi-
> vidual incompleteness. In the community—be it family,
> nation, or humanity itself—the individual involves himself
> in something beyond his own person in order to answer his
> quest for a final meaning to his existence. Although the
> ultimate answer does not reside in human groups, but rather
> in the Creator himself, still much of what is essentially
> human can be known through participation in a commun-
> ity.[25]

These newer ideas about community led Hatfield to reexamine
his approach to power and Christian leadership. To him, the
American notion of power—appropriately symbolized by idolatry
of the presidency—has little substance in terms of the biblical
concept of power. American politicians, in love with their own
positions of influence, are unable to ask forgiveness or even to
admit wrongdoing. Hatfield knew of just one solution—"to give
our lives over to a higher power, the power of God's love in
Christ."[26] Only such a vision of power would create an attitude of
true humility in the Christian leader.

Conventional political wisdom, the senator said, holds that leadership is power. "Power is something you acquire; power is some-

thing you use to manipulate people and build a political base; power is domination...."[27] Why have American politicians developed that view of leadership? Because of the expectations of the citizenry. For example, Hatfield feels that Americans expect the president somehow to embody attributes of bishop, tribal chief, the American Dream, manipulator of the economy, and our security blanket. "We expect him to do all these things as well as be a soothsayer, to allay our fears, to calm our hearts.... We have created an idolatry of power."[28]

Such a concept is wrong—not only scripturally but also constitutionally, the senator contended: "'We the people' is the preamble. That's where the sovereignty of the nation is, not in the government."[29]

Why have "we the people" created this idolatry of high office? Because "we have let the wellsprings of deep spiritual faith in our lives run dry," Hatfield asserted. "Man will always have a god.... If God is not the source of his ultimate allegiance, man ... will worship other people, or his country, or institutions, or money, or power...."[30] Since the solution is spiritual, each of us must "confess our personal and national sins, and ask for God's mercy and forgiveness."[31]

Because the Christian must mold his life after that of Christ, Hatfield contended, the individual must understand

> that leadership is not the protection of power, but rather the commitment to service.... It is an openness, a candor, a humility, a sacrifice. [The Christian leader] places the well-being of the other ahead of his own....
>
> Political wisdom of the day teaches precisely the opposite—to save one's life, he takes, he squeezes, he grabs, he accumulates, he surrounds himself with protection....
>
> We must turn from this idolatry of power to the vision of one who is a servant leader.[32]

The senator accepted the fact that nonbelievers would find it difficult to understand this vision of leadership. But it disturbed him greatly that Christians didn't realize their mandate, for Christians "are called to a renewal of society, to corporate repentance, to justice, to relief of suffering, 'to proclaim the release of the captives, to set at liberty those who are oppressed,' as the Scripture states. That must be the shape of the evangelistic mission in our time and our land."[33]

Just as Hatfield expected Christian leaders to be different, he also expected Christian institutions, especially the church, to operate differently from secular organizations. For example, an Anabaptist interpretation of the doctrine of church-state separation strengthened his previous opposition to lobbying by the institutional church. Lobbying might compromise the church's unique prophetic role:

> I do not believe that the church as an institution should attempt an active role in policy decisions of government. For, once those decisions were made, the church would then be in a position of having to sanction the government itself as being holy and just. But the church does have the obligation to mobilize its own members and communicants to an awareness of the dimensions of the problems around them. . . .[34]

Hatfield had other reasons for opposing political lobbying by arms of the institutional church. Ineffectiveness was one of them. With the exception of the Quakers, the senator dismissed other denominational and interdenominational organizations as "rank amateurs" in political lobbying. Recently he has been especially critical of the National Council of Churches, labeling it Capitol Hill's most ineffective lobby.[35]

Even an "effective" religious lobby would be unacceptable to Hatfield, though, for that would mean copying the methods of the world. The goal of lobbyists is to manipulate their congressional contacts. As a "Christian politician," Hatfield was a popular target for religious lobbyists—and thus was sensitive to such manipulation. He doubted whether lobbyists for institutions like the National Council of Churches truly represented the desires of their constituents. His Baptist congregationalism and radical Anabaptism made him suspicious of attempts to integrate faith and politics via lobbying pressure.

Another important issue highlighting Hatfield's radical Anabaptism is abortion. From the start, he questioned what "unlimited" abortion would do to the moral foundation of American society. After a 1973 U.S. Supreme Court decision loosened restrictions on abortion, Hatfield, Sen. James Buckley (a Conservative from New York), and four others proposed a constitutional amendment banning abortion except when the pregnancy endangered the mother's life and when conception resulted from rape.

While supporters of the feminist movement and assorted political liberals attacked this legislation because of its ostensible narrowness and repressiveness, Hatfield argued forcefully that—quite the opposite—the legislation was truly progressive. He based his argument on the truth that all human life is valuable and sacred, and turned to science and Christian ethics to justify his position. He felt science clearly proved that life began the moment the embryo became implanted on the wall of the uterus. He opposed the attempt to reduce abortion to a question of individual conscience as well as the Supreme Court's effort to impose "legal categories" on an issue about which there was no basic moral or scientific disagreement.

On the ethical side, Hatfield rejected the charge that supporters of the legislation were trying to impose a narrow religious view on everyone else. He quickly differentiated between church doctrines and universally accepted moral principles: "The right to life is a basic human right, protected by the Declaration of Independence, the Constitution, and the Declaration of Human Rights of the United Nations. A church's assertion of this right does not make the issue a religious one."[36]

Although Hatfield sympathized with women whose pregnancies had caused them emotional trauma and sociological as well as legal discrimination, he argued that

> despite the harshness of such truths, these are not the criteria for determining when human life begins, or whether the existence of that life has value.
>
> . . . the crimes of society do not exempt an individual from moral responsibility. . . . Sociological tragedy does not alter the biological reality of a life's existence.

Further; I cannot condone any liberation movement that demands the sacrifice of innocent human life.

The humanization of mankind will never come through condoning the slaughter of unborn life. Gandhi's words apply directly: "The means is the ends in the making."[37]

The senator considered abortion a continuation of the ethic of violence which had plagued American society since the outbreak of the Vietnam War:

Abortion is a form of violence. That is the undeniable reality. It is the destruction of life. It furthers the dehumanization of life. It cheapens life.

So we face a complex, troublesome issue. And what do we . . . do? Resort to violence once again. . . . Violence is no solution. We have had enough. It is time it all stopped.

Let us believe in life. Let us nourish life. Let us commit ourselves to life.[38]

Abortion was particularly repulsive to Hatfield when suggested as a means of dealing with overcrowding and hunger in underdeveloped countries. In a comprehensive 1975 statement, he suggested five alternatives for controlling the world's population explosion: education in childbirth and sexuality, family planning programs (contraception), liberalized adoption procedures, more adequate social services (increased standards of living), and new medical research. Of course, even such a "comprehensive" plan did not have all the answers, but it was a courageous call to biblical wisdom in a difficult area of modern life.

In sum, an examination of the senator's "prophetic" theology reveals that he essentially fused many basic elements of faith and politics during the late 1960s and early 1970s. Moreover, this synthesis, extending far beyond the horizon of mainstream evangelicalism, also created the foundation for a more detailed program of political and economic reformation. As we will see in succeeding chapters, little escaped his attention. Hatfield busily attacked many of the structural weaknesses of the American system, proposing legislative and other remedies to move the country along the path toward justice and compassion. His unique Christian vision provided refreshing and insightful approaches to such diverse concerns as participatory democracy at the local level, redesigning the federal tax system, and world hunger. Seldom has the United States witnessed such a comprehensive effort by one politician to reform the system.

"Redoing the System"

> It is time to "redo" the system from the bottom up. We can do it. We can make a substantial simplification which also brings reform—for the poor, the elderly, for the [small] business entrepreneur, and for the overburdened and over-bothered middle class.[1]

THE GUNS-AND-BUTTER prosperity spawned during the wartime 1960s was great. Joe M. Class and his wife, Jane, set forth like millions of others to slice off their own wedge of the Great American Pie. Capitalizing on surging property values during the early 1970s, they sold their small home for $28,000—double what they had paid eight years earlier.

But their handsome new home with fireplace, four bedrooms, and double garage cost $60,000. Their monthly house payments, $160 a month previously, ballooned to $410. Because city buses didn't serve their new neighborhood, Joe and Jane bought a second automobile. Payment: $140 a month. To finance the fruits of their new prosperity, Jane went back to work.

The local school had been a key factor in their choice of a new neighborhood. Located just two blocks away, it was close enough that Susie and Tom could walk home even in bad weather. The building was modern and well equipped and safe. The teachers were well trained, talented, and had sparked both children to new academic heights.

Then—boom! A federal judge ordered the school system to correct racial imbalance in some schools by busing. Tom and Susie were among those selected by computer for the cross-town busing program. They ended up an hour away at their old school—an aging, deteriorating structure. Real estate taxes soared, partly to pay for buses and drivers.

Then came the energy crisis, which—to Class and his friends—looked more like a Great American Rip-off they were powerless to fight. Watergate confirmed the Classes' opinion of politicians. The final frustration came one night when Jane guided her loaded cart to the checkout lane of the supermarket. To meet her budget, she stocked up on hamburger, hot dogs, macaroni and cheese. Just ahead of her a woman, her cart stocked with fancy cuts of beef and fresh pastries, paid her bill with food stamps.

With four children of his own, plus a home in suburban Maryland, Senator Hatfield well understood the frustrations encountered by the mythical Joe M. Class family. Not being a man of wealth, Hatfield took to the lecture circuit to help meet his financial obligations. But he sensed far greater frustrations than financial ones, particularly disillusionment with the "system"—the unresponsiveness, the nosiness (a Social Security number on every form, a questionnaire in every mailbox), the runaround ("I just work here; I don't make the rules").

Hatfield's answer to the Great American Nightmare was a series of stunning, interrelated reforms where political power would be redirected, a restoration of the "sovereignty of the people through powerful, community-based self-government."[2] Democratization through decentralized "neighborhood government" was his overarching goal.

The origin of Hatfield's reform proposals, especially neighborhood government ideas, can be traced, in part, to his own Christian experiences:

> It comes out of my desire to see every part of society, every person in society, recognized and his opportunity enhanced to become an integral and relevant part of a community. I discovered community through my Christian commitment, where I could very openly be and say and do without any defenses, without any fear. That is a different kind of community than the neighborhood government but it gave me a model, an appreciation, a stimulus, an understanding of what community could be. It gave me a strong motivation in the political field to help move people into this kind of

neighborhood community relationship. It can become the ground of a new political order and more authentic early American political order vis-a-vis the town hall where people felt their voice counted, their vote counted, their life was to be defended and protected as much as the wealthy or the big corporation.

But government isn't the only villain. The U.S. economic system also alienates the individual. In the *Ripon Forum* (January 1973), Hatfield contended that economic centralization has only compounded the frustration of the individual. Despite America's affluency, the gap remains substantial between the rich and the poor. Uncharted economic growth has seriously depleted many of our resources, at severe ecological cost. Much like big government, he continued, big corporations dominate the economic scene:

> Today, 1.1 percent of all the nation's corporations control 81.5 percent of all corporate assets. Such centralization is eroding the values and contributions of small business, and also tends . . . to increase the problems of worker alienation and consumer distrust.
>
> In short, we are regarding "consumerism" as the end and goal of our economic system, instead of regarding that system as the means to provide citizens with productive, creative, and fulfilling opportunities for work. Thus, we end up with enormous waste, planned obsolescence, make-believe work, feather-bedding mindless gadgetry, and meaningless labor, all in order to fuel our increasing rates of consumption. . . . We now should re-define the meaning of work, and the goals of our economic system. . . . We must come to see work, not as a dehumanizing monotonous activity, but as the right to express one's gifts and abilities as he participates in society's economic abundance. . . .
>
> We must then encourage a revival of the crafts, of the artisan, of "cottage industries," of the shopkeeper, and the small entrepreneur.

A few months later (Aug. 26, 1973) Hatfield, writing in the *Washington Post*, proposed "five ways to rebuild confidence" after Watergate. A call for neighborhood government was one of the five. The other four radical reforms would remold social institutions and enable people to regain a measure of control over their lives. He criticized both the Democratic and Republican parties for lacking the wisdom and courage to develop similar creative proposals.

First, Hatfield called for a constitutional amendment "requiring separate election of the president, the vice-president and various heads of cabinet departments" (i.e., those cabinet officers whose duties were confined to domestic issues). Such a system, Hatfield suggested, would provide a "creative tension" in the executive department, making it more responsive to the people. In essence, the senator called for a "plural executive," spreading among several elected officials the power now concentrated in the office of the president.

Second, he proposed a massive overhaul of the federal bureaucracy, reducing the work force and significantly revising civil service regulations. "After three years in the civil service [employees] have acquired virtual life tenure," he wrote. "... One of the rarest events in Washington is the firing of a civil servant for slothfulness." To deal with the problem, the senator suggested a limit of five to nine years in federal service—with some flexibility to allow "committed civil servants who have proven their worth" to continue on in their positions. Only such drastic revision of civil service, he believed, would overcome bureaucratic inertia and the self-serving ends of workers whose very existence made the government less responsive. (Hatfield didn't overlook the inertia problem in the legislative branch, either. During his first Senate term—during which only one Republican, Jacob Javits of New York, introduced more bills—Hatfield sought a limit on congressional seniority. He introduced a bill requiring a two-year "sabbatical leave" for representatives and senators who had served for twelve consecutive years.)

Third, as a companion to political decentralization under neighborhood government, Hatfield asked for parallel decentralization in the economic community. Such a fundamental reordering of the economic system would transform the manner in which wealth is accumulated and controlled. Much like big government, the senator asserted, large

> economic conglomerates are prone to attempt to mold public policy.... Fundamental steps must be taken to accomplish the deconglomeration of the American economy. Then, in every possible way, people must be offered a personal stake, or share, in our nation's economy. Today, the wealthiest 10 per cent of all American families receive 29 per cent of all income and hold 56 per cent of all wealth.... But the ultimate solution is not any simple scheme to distribute the wealth; rather, the fundamental challenge is to distribute the ownership and control over the accumulation of wealth.

To secure greater economic equity—without increasing the power of the state—he had specific suggestions: reviving the family farm by banning from farming any businesses with assets greater than $3 million; encouraging small business by making the first $25,000 of corporate profits tax free; strictly enforcing and initiating antitrust laws against both big business and big labor; and supporting employee stock ownership plans.

Fourth, Hatfield outlined a "fundamentally new approach to simplify and reform" the federal income-tax system for individuals to provide equity and fairness. He called this reform measure "Simpliform," and he pointed out good reasons why the tax system needed to be simplified: "From a one-paragraph amendment to the Constitution, the income tax has emerged as a hydra-headed monster that now takes more than a 6-foot bookshelf to contain its laws and regulations." If Simpliform, and the other measures, were seriously considered by Congress, the senator felt resulting legislation could "restore the relevance and meaning to citizenship and political life in America."

In the fall of 1973 Hatfield introduced his first Simpliform tax bill and his first comprehensive Neighborhood Government Act (introduced in abbreviated form in 1971). Both bills reflected his disillusionment with corporate capitalism and a materialistic society. Because of the enormous power of corporations, Hatfield realized that neighborhood government legislation depended on a Simpliform-like restructuring of tax laws. Neighborhood governments couldn't flourish in America without redistribution of wealth. In Hatfield's mind, the revenue sharing plan of 1972, under which the federal government returns tax money to state and local governments, wouldn't do the job:

> [Under] tax revenue sharing, after the federal government takes from the people, it gives back to the people. [But] once they yield that money to the federal government, they've yielded power and they never get it back, even though they may get tokens back. They're getting their own money back after it's been filtered through a bureaucracy, and the handling costs have been very high.

The senator believed that revenue sharing programs reversed the direction power should flow in effective democracy. Rather than local residents deciding how to use their own funds under revenue sharing, localities received money with federal limitations on how to spend it.

He introduced Simpliform in September 1973, and the proposal—when contrasted with complex income tax regulations—is remarkable. Under Simpliform, employers would withhold ten percent of each employee's income. Individuals then would pay a progressively based surtax on income—wages, gifts, prizes, interest, dividends, etc.—exceeding that ten percent. As initially formulated, the surtax would range from five percent on incomes from $10,000 to $15,000 up to forty percent on incomes over $1 million.[3] Most taxpayers would have to do no more than attach withholding forms to a one-page tax form and fill in four figures: total income, gross tax, credit for personal exemptions (adults only), and net tax (or refund) due. There would be no deductions!

Hatfield felt that Simpliform would accomplish four things: first, simplifying a system which baffles and angers most taxpayers; second, raising enough money to meet federal budget requirements; third, retaining the spirit of older income tax laws—requiring payment based on the ability to pay; fourth, decreasing the amount of income tax paid by eighty-five to ninety percent of Americans. (Lower taxes would be realized even by most of those who painstakingly itemize deductions under the present system.)

Even though the Simpliform measure appears to be equitable and simple, the senator knew the bill had little chance of immediate approval. It was too radical and, he suggested, too sensible, for Congress to accept. So far the proposal hasn't advanced beyond the Senate Finance Committee. There has been little media notice, aside from the *Christian Science Monitor*[4] and Oregon newspapers. The educational task is massive: not only must he convince those at the lower end of the income spectrum that change, in this case, would be good—he also must overcome resistance from the wealthy, who benefit from loopholes in the present system. It will take considerable political muscle to succeed, because both the economic and political establishments figure they are better off under the current plan. Even though individual maximum tax rates extend as high as seventy percent now, loopholes and deductions allow many of the wealthy to pay substantially less. Simpliform's maximum of fifty percent offers no loopholes.

Hatfield called the comprehensive Neighborhood Government Act, introduced Oct. 1, 1973, the "cornerstone of my whole domestic philosophy."[5] The focus of that domestic philosophy was on the local community. The bill set forth the groundwork for a participatory democracy with political power stripped from Washington and placed at the local level. The great need is to make government more responsive to its citizens:

> If America is to resist the forces that are nibbling away at our individual freedom, a dynamic political movement must arise to limit the powers of big government, big labor and big business. It must be a movement committed to reshaping and decentralizing the institutions of power in society. . . . The only way to restore the people's trust in the institutions of power is to break open new avenues for the

people to participate directly in those institutions and remold them. . . .

This program of decentralization and constitutionalism
would move decisively to limit the powers of the presidency,
to replace bureaucratic government—federal, state or
local—with "neighborhood government," to restore an
economic environment that encourages small entrepreneur-
ship and insures corporate competition and accountability,
and to assure the privacy and autonomy of the individual
American.[6]

In the senator's view, most citizens were alienated from their
own government. After decades of unsuccessfully trying to participate meaningfully in their own government, Hatfield felt that most
Americans had simply given up. Their frustrations, plus a growing
cynicism about politicians and political corruption, combined to
drive a wedge between citizens and government. As the alienation
and apathy of Americans increased, so had the power of government. By dropping out of the political process, the average citizen
had strengthened the federal bureaucracy by default. When intro-
ducing his Neighborhood Government Act, Hatfield did not

dispute the need for the Federal Government to take dramatic and forceful action in response to many of the crises that
we face. But I do maintain that the goals of social and human
liberation—the freeing of each citizen from social, political,
economic, and technological oppression, and the liberating
of his spirit for creative self-fulfillment—will never be
wrought exclusively through the means of the Federal Government's centralized power.[7]

Despite the good that many federal relief and renewal programs
promised, Hatfield felt that they not only didn't achieve their
goals, but in some cases even contributed to the deterioration of
the target communities. He attacked "Great Society" programs for
falsely raising the expectations of persons living in areas pinpointed
for "renewal." In introductory comments about the Neighborhood
Government Act, the senator cited a detailed study of the Bed-
ford-Stuyvesant poverty area of New York City. That neighborhood was the focal point of innumerable antipoverty programs

during the 1960s. Regardless of the programs, earned income of residents declined from 1959 to 1969. The study concluded that if residents' financial resources had remained in the community— instead of being siphoned off via taxes, banks, and corporations— there would have been enough money to finance many, perhaps all, of the community's own programs. In other words, had the community been left alone, it would have been better off!

Hatfield sadly concluded that the enormous growth of power had turned the federal government from an institution of "servant-hood" to one of "domination." He saw neighborhood government as a means of reviving the concept of "political servanthood":

> . . . as I conceive of it, neighborhood government is groups of individuals living within common geographical areas with participatory forms of government. The citizens would have ultimate control over their own services. . . . All of this, of course, would have to be in concert with State and Federal laws as well as within the guidelines of the Constitution.[8]

The proposal provided for various means of financing neighborhood governments, or "corporations" as he called them. Individuals could elect to send ten to eighty percent of their federal income taxes as tax credits to their local neighborhood corporations. Poorer people could contribute a higher percentage of income than the rich, thereby hopefully equalizing the effect of wealth on a neighborhood. Individuals and financial institutions outside the corporation could also contribute funds. Further, the bill provided for direct grants to neighborhoods—equal to the total nonfederal taxes paid by all neighborhood residents.

Under the bill, the secretary of the treasury would decide the boundaries of specific neighborhood corporations. (Hatfield suggested natural geographic boundaries as the best.) The secretary would also determine whether a sufficient number of residents of a neighborhood had volunteered and were qualified to form a neighborhood corporation. (The senator suggested seventy percent participation as a workable figure.)

What activities could neighborhoods handle for themselves? Hatfield recommended an astonishing range of local concerns, including

> day-care centers, drug-abuse centers, halfway houses, and
> outpatient health clinics. . . . Parks and recreation centers,
> welfare programs, cooperative stores, banks and credit un-
> ions, and local police forces and fire departments, all meet-
> ing established standards, are all possible if the
> people . . . are given direct control of tax monies that are so
> often wasted.
>
> These neighborhoods should have some right and power
> to decide where a city's freeways are built. Local com-
> munities . . . must assume the power to determine how their
> land should be utilized, and how their ecology should be
> protected.[9]

Two major components of neighborhood government in Hatfield's
mind, are penal systems and schools. To make the criminal rehabilitation system responsive and effective would require community involvement. The senator expressed similar thoughts
about neighborhood control of the educational system—including
financing, teaching, and administering the schools. Neighborhoods would decide for themselves if they wanted to be part of a
larger educational system.

In Hatfield's view, only a decentralized community on the order
of neighborhood government would be likely to prevent national
disaster:

> If we cannot change our institutions, if we are irrevocably
> wedded to the past, we may face an Orwellian future of our
> own making. The Orwellian future would be a simple one,
> devoid of personal response and initiative. The
> people . . . are as dead as their leaders and they embody a
> society that has no future.
>
> Only by renewing the spirit of man . . . can America move
> into its third century of life with . . . the promise and fascina-
> tion of freedom.[10]

Without decentralization, Hatfield feared further advance of a
secular totalitarianism which would thwart efforts to express individual religious diversity and communal vitality. He was especially
eager to see that Christianity flourished, because he considered
Christians the "salt" of America—the force preserving the society

from collapse and pointing the way toward reformation. By basing his ideas of community upon the worth of the individual, he sought to avoid the extremes of naked individualism and socialism.

Hatfield's idea of neighborhood government is similar to his view of a family:

> The family is strongest where each individual functions as part of that unit. The small neighborhood government [unit] is a vital element because each person in that community is functional and has power. The state is but the instrumentality through which group life is facilitated, and the state, therefore, is the agent of the people. Once people come together in a group action where there is a strong sense of individual importance, concern, and compassion, there is a meaningful role they can play toward someone else. There begins an environment in which a Christian ethic, a Christian morality, can be introduced and can take hold and become a reality.

Hatfield's neighborhood government plan is indeed radically unconventional. As such, it transcends conservatism and liberalism—both religious and secular. But what problems are presented by the neighborhood government concept? "The biggest obstacle," according to Hatfield, "is the federal government itself, not wanting to give up its command of the resources [to] the people."[11] In addition, talk of a "town hall" participatory democracy sounds simplistic and unrealistic to modern ears. Partly because of such criticism, Hatfield wisely suggested pilot programs to establish neighborhood corporations and examine the unforeseen problems that might surface.

There are other shortcomings. The federal government would play a far less active domestic role, primarily creating minimum guidelines for neighborhood corporations. Yet the senator makes few suggestions as to what these guidelines might include. That lack of definite standards has prompted liberals to be wary of neighborhood government. No doubt many liberals feel that hard-fought victories for civil and social rights might be jeopardized under a neighborhood approach without specific legal minimum standards.

Some critics suggest that neighborhood government would merely add one more level of government to the several already existing. How would conflicts between neighborhoods and city governments be resolved? Hatfield seems to suggest a gradual withering away of existing municipal governments—an event not calculated to please local politicians.

Conservatives, such as syndicated columnist George F. Will, are sharply critical of Hatfield's reform proposals, including neighborhood government. Will labeled Hatfield's "five ways to rebuild confidence" (in the senator's *Washington Post* article) as "unexceptional," "uninspired," a "mishmash of new words and old pieties," and "dizzy" (in the case of neighborhood government and separate election of vice-presidents and cabinet officers). "Hatfield simply does not understand that government treats us as *citizens*, not neighbors," Will wrote, "because our problems link us to many millions of citizens with whom we cannot be neighborly in a continental nation."[12]

Will's critique cannot be ignored, for Hatfield's approach—drawing from Hoover and radical Anabaptism—*is* a little anti-political. Despite his radical and exciting call for decentralized government, Hatfield lacks the important key marked "cultural pluralism." Such a key would provide him with a fuller definition of community. His definition remains basically geographical, downplaying "religion" and "ethnicity" and "ideology." Churches, ethnic communities, and ideological groups (or any combination thereof) are envisioned by Hatfield as playing, at best, supportive roles in a system of pre-existing, geographically defined neighborhood corporations. Ironically, Hatfield's program inhibits the full expression of community, for communities are rooted, by definition, in religion, ethnicity, and ideology. Failure to recognize this is leading to great frustration and resentment in American society.

Actually, cultural pluralism could be experienced through Hatfield's neighborhood government, because it is not prohibited per se. But Hatfield, and no doubt others, feel that divisiveness would be the result of a decentralized system based on religion and related forces. One can argue, though, that only *through* recognition of real diversity can the system (and nation) be healed!

What about evangelicals? How have they reacted? Evangelical publications have paid little heed to Hatfield's political prophecy. How have individual evangelicals responded? "I don't know that I've had any response from evangelicals," Hatfield replies. "It's a little far out for them." More likely, most evangelicals have never heard of neighborhood government—a sad commentary on the lack of communication (even from Hatfield) and political community among evangelicals. Much more dialogue is needed, not only about Hatfield's remarkable proposals, but about all suggestions for mapping out normative political direction for American society.

Tweedledee, Tweedledum

Our wealth and our standard of living is a cause of endless other problems such as our energy crisis, the ruining of our physical resources, the ruining of our physical environment, and our outright monopoly on the world's basic resources.[1]

OF ALL THE frustrations stemming from corporate or bureaucratic ranks in recent years, perhaps the most vexing to our suburban friend, Joe M. Class, has been the energy crisis. Class and other Oregonians remember the trying moments after the 1973 Arab-Israeli War when eleven Arab countries shut off oil shipments to the United States (and other nations friendly to Israel). Class and his friends could buy gasoline only on odd or even days (depending on the last digit of their vehicle license plate). Often they languished in hour-long lines at service stations, inching forward (and burning fuel) a car's length at a time toward the gasoline pumps. Remembering that pre-"crisis" gasoline cost about 38 cents a gallon, the Classes watched with alarm—and no small measure of suspicion—as the price zoomed past 40, past 50, even past 60 cents per gallon. Oil-company rationalizations sounded hollow.

Those were difficult times for the Pacific Northwest. Not only were fossil fuels in short supply, but drought substantially diminished the flow and hydroelectric power production of the mighty Columbia River. Oregon Gov. Tom McCall declared an emergency in the fall of 1973; power suppliers trimmed allocations to some industrial and commercial users. Oregon's nights were dark, as the state banned highway and commercial display lighting. Class, and many others, lost several days of work because of power cutbacks. Those temporary layoffs, coming as they did when in-

113

flated prices already had sliced buying power, crimped the Classes'
budget and the state's economy.

Warm, heavy rains in January 1974 filled the rivers, ending the
drought and the hydroelectric problem but not the overall energy
crisis. And the frustrations remained, even about little things.
Class was annoyed because he had to convert a corner of his garage
into a warehouse for the beverage business. Oregon's "bottle bill,"
which took effect in October 1972, required deposits on all soft-
drink, malt-beverage, and mineral-water containers. Class wasn't
convinced this helped the Oregon economy, but he conceded that
it did beautify the countryside a bit.

Class didn't know what to think of President Nixon's comprehensive "answer" to the national energy crisis—Project Independence, a plan to make the United States self-sufficient in
energy by 1980. The president and his energy advisers called for
more sacrifices on the part of our mythical friend and his fellow
Americans: lower speed limits, lower home thermostats, no
gasoline sales on Sunday, reduced air travel, relaxed environmental standards, perhaps even gasoline rationing.

That stuff was tough for Class to swallow, especially after his
neighbor showed him a *Wall Street Journal* article detailing the
burgeoning profits for the energy companies. "What can we do?"
Class complained to his wife. "The politicians are in league with the
oil companies. . . . Turn the rascals out? It won't make any difference. Voting never does. We're never given a real choice. [Class
hadn't bothered to vote for several years.] Find me one—just one
politician—Democrat or Republican, who is on *our* side."

Upon investigation, Class was encouraged to find that his senior
senator, Mark Hatfield, was skeptical and frustrated, too. On
March 11, 1974, Hatfield warned on the Senate floor that Project
Independence was misleading, promising more than it could deliver to the average American:

> The fact that it takes energy to extract energy . . . is a crucial
> consideration to which our energy planners and economic
> advisers have not paid attention. We should be asking—and
> finding out—just how many Btu's are burned up in making
> 10 Btu's of energy available. . . . We need to assess the Presi-

dent's "Project Independence" immediately in terms of what we are going to expend for what we intend to get. . . . The major new energy processes being developed to replace our conventional sources [like nuclear reactors and shale extraction] will require more energy to get the energy available to the consumer. . . . We can soon expect this phenomenon of declining net energy percentage to become the principal cause of inflation, eclipsing all the other inflationary pressures. . . . An inappropriate energy policy, one that does not take net energy into account, will be felt in terms of a general economic crisis rather than in terms of the energy crisis that lies at its base. . . .

Suppose that for every 10 energy units of . . . oil shale proposed as an energy source, there were required 9 units of energy to mine, process, concentrate, transport, and meet the environmental requirements. Such a shale reserve would deliver only one-tenth as much net energy and last one-tenth as long. . . . We are getting a phony picture today.[2]

Hatfield was thus arguing for meaningful reform, where the end product was a gain in net energy, not a loss.

Such a program could only be built upon a foundation of clear thinking about our whole American style of living. But clear thinking was the exception rather than the rule. In that same Senate speech Hatfield spelled out five common and dangerous misconceptions about U.S. energy problems frequently held by citizens (like Joe M. Class): (1) Never mind the warnings; we really have unlimited fuel to power a consumption-oriented society. (2) Antidevelopment tactics of the environmentalists caused the energy crisis. (3) Population increases, not higher per-capita consumption, caused the energy crisis. (4) The crisis is temporary, prompted primarily by the Arab oil embargo of 1973. (5) Experts in government and the academic community will somehow provide the wherewithal to deal with our problems and guide us past the danger of depression.

The senator adamantly opposed plans for gasoline rationing, arguing that such a short-term option would only increase bureaucracy and place an unfair burden on individual drivers (particularly in large states like Oregon). Instead, Hatfield offered a radical two-dimension solution for the energy crisis.

First, he contended that decentralization of the energy industry was essential. He recommended ending the oil depletion allowance, breaking up large companies' monopoly on market operations, discontinuing tax credits on foreign oil royalties, and—if the other suggestions were implemented—deregulation of the entire industry. These unconventional proposals contrasted sharply with the main tenets of the National Energy Emergency Act of 1973, which delegated considerable congressional power to the president without making the necessary structural reforms. "When we in Congress get into a crunch . . . all the rhetoric about congressional responsibility goes out the window in our eagerness to pass the ball to the president," the senator said. "Congress need not become [an administrating branch of government], but it should set policy."[3]

Second, Hatfield suggested a four-pronged, long-term national energy plan providing: (1) reduced consumption of nonrenewable energy and careful examination of nuclear energy; (2) a reduction in total energy use; (3) better use of our energy in producing food; and (4) a deliberate move toward a "steady state" (i.e., unchanging) economy! His plea for a steady state economy is closely related to his suggestion that the nation adopt an "energy budget" as well as a fiscal budget. Such an energy budget, considering the energy cost of producing more energy, would enable planners to smooth the path toward an era of limited energy and a steady state economy.

Other politicians and social theorists have advanced some of the above recommendations, but few, at least in establishment circles, have fused them into a comprehensive plan designed to redirect our whole economy. For example, what other major party politician has seriously proposed that America seek a steady state economy, built upon a gross national product which (after adjustments for inflation and population) would not increase at all?

In the area of environmental protection, Hatfield is quick to point out that he is not a Johnny-come-lately. Despite the national reputation gained by Oregon in McCall's two terms (1967-75), Hatfield contends that the groundwork was laid long ago:

The state of Oregon has had a history of environmental concern, based upon the great Oz West who started our state along these lines. Some timber legislation and conservation practices put Oregon far ahead of all other states in the '20s, '30s, and '40s. . . . It was in my administration that we took on Portland for pollution of the Willamette River. Everybody said, "Oh, we can't tackle the big municipality of Portland—that's suicide." We laid it on Portland. We challenged Portland to stop polluting. [Some corporations] wanted to do some exploration of offshore oil possibilities while I was governor. We called together the Fish Commission, the Game Commission, the Izaak Walton League and the citizens groups, and we said: "Now, let us look at the possibility of exploration. If there is a feasibility of exploration, then let us put the rules and regulations so clearly that we are going to protect our vast resources, [our] environment." And we put representatives out there in the boats while the exploration was going on to make sure that the regulations were enforced. We worked together.

As senator, Hatfield has been more aggressive in the area of environmental protection than he had been as governor. In the Senate he sponsored or co-sponsored numerous antipollution measures. One, for example, dealt with noise pollution. Others emulated Oregon's famous bottle bill, banning the sale and shipment of nonreturnable beverage containers nationally. The ill-fated national bottle bill illustrates the senator's utter dismay at the distorted values of a materialistic society. Said Hatfield: "The people of Oregon have shown that we [as a nation] can reject the throwaway society exemplified by snap-tab, flip-top, throwaway cans and bottles."[4] When constituents like Joe M. Class expressed annoyance at the inconvenience of such legislation, Hatfield urged patience, arguing that the long-term effect would be a net gain in both jobs and energy.

Hatfield's American Forestry Acts of 1971 and 1973 sought to provide funds for improving the quality of public and private forests—for recreational use as well as timber production and preserving the environment. Speaking in the Senate in 1971, he declared that the forestry act seeks

> to institute programs designed to reforest and restore the
> quality of public and private forest lands; to enhance and
> expand recreational opportunity on such lands; to provide
> financial incentives to improve management of State and
> private forest lands; to establish a Federal forest lands man-
> agement fund; to facilitate public participation in Federal
> resources management; and to enhance the quality of the
> environment. . . .[5]

The forestry acts made little progress in the Senate. The U.S.
Department of the Interior and other federal agencies opposed the
bills, contending that existing legislation and practices accomplished all that was proposed in the new forestry acts.

Hatfield further sympathized with Joe M. Class' complaint that
the political system was unresponsive. Yet Hatfield's evolution as a
political maverick—as evidenced by Vietnam—and the loose party
structure in Oregon meant that for him conventional representa-
tion was inadequate; he believed his responsibility was

> to help create public opinion, not merely to react to
> it. . . . I'm going to vote my conscience. Even if every person
> in Oregon was on the other side, I'd vote my convictions.
> . . . But if I stopped at that point, then that would be the
> height of hypocrisy and the autocratic mentality. That would
> be no different than being a king. . . .
>
> I vote my convictions; then I go forth and stand account-
> able for that position to the people in our state. . . . I must
> answer. So that puts it back into the context of democratic
> thinking. . . .[6]

What happens when there is a conflict between conscience and
constituents? As noted in chapter five, Hatfield faced such a dilemma shortly after becoming governor. The question was capital
punishment, which Hatfield opposes. Should he commute the
death sentence of a convicted murderer, or should he abide by the
will of the people (as expressed through the courts and state
legislators) and allow the man to die? After hours of anguish,
Governor Hatfield decided that the will of the people must be
honored.

Later, as senator, he reassessed that decision:

. . . if faced with that decision today, a decade and a half later,
I question whether my choice would be the same. Now, by
acknowledging as a higher duty the prior dictates of my
conscience and my faith rather than my obligations to the
majority will of the people, I might rather render first unto
God than unto Caesar. . . .

To what extent should a politician in a representative
democracy guide his or her actions by the popular opinion of
the people? . . .

Faithfulness to our Lord is the ultimate test of our actions.
. . . Ours . . . is not the responsibility to "make history.". . .
We know that history's true purposes are brought closer to
their fulfillment not by our allegiance to some ideology, but
through our faithfulness to Jesus Christ.[7]

Such thoughts, and the senator's growing radicalization in many
other areas, prompted considerable inner turmoil. Should he work
to revive a healthy two-party system—including a dynamic Republican Party—or should he find a new, different system that might
be more representative of the citizenry?

During most of his first Senate term he believed that the two-
party apparatus and the Republican Party could be politically
representative if they functioned openly and equitably. Approxi-
mately 1970, however, he shifted gears, recognizing that the political party system was functioning improperly. The turning point
came when Hatfield attacked the Nixon Administration's plan for a
"Southern strategy" to revive the sagging fortunes of the Republican Party. To Hatfield, that idea was outrageous

when you consider that that type of rightward movement
excludes the black people, it excludes the young people, it
excludes most of those within the small business groups,
perhaps, and labor, and ethnic groups of all kinds . . . you
can't be a national party on that kind of narrow base.[8]

The senator contended that a "Southern strategy" ran counter to
the principles of historic Republicanism, especially the radical
Republicans of the 1860s and 1870s. He identified with those early
radical Republicans because of their openness to blacks, their
opposition to inordinate presidential power, and their critical at-

titude toward the military. Although he remains a Republican, he reached the point several years ago of declaring that the two major parties are "in their last days."

The combined impact of Hatfield's disillusionment, his prophetic Christianity, and his creative approach to radical political reform provides two practical options: multiparty politics and political "functionalism." He doesn't consider the multiparty representative systems of western Europe to be appropriate for the United States—despite his conviction about the "last days" of the two major parties. What about a parliamentary legislative system, in contrast to a congressional system, perhaps modeled after that of England? "I have a warm reaction to that," the senator responds. "I don't think it's very near, but I do feel that it would be perhaps a better system than what we have."

What can we look for in the near future? The two-party system, Hatfield believes, is in a state of transition

> void of design or strategy. It just happens. We're in a state of flux. I think the two-party system could represent—but is not—the broad interests of the people. The two parties are becoming an ornament in the minds of many people, an ornament that's terribly unimportant. But I'm not sure that those who call themselves independents have really defined themselves as much as they have reacted to the two parties. Increasing numbers of people look upon the two parties as Tweedledee, Tweedledum, so totally pluralistic in each of the parties that it is difficult to get a clear philosophical distinction.

Thus, "functionalism," the senator predicts, is the coming American compromise between the two-party approach and the European multiparty system:

> I think there's going to be a sort of functionalism—a new functionalism that may develop, in which your [Ralph] Nader group, your Common Cause, gather together on common purpose on this issue and regroup, say, on some other issue. But they don't want to be locked in to being a Republican or a Democrat. I think they want the freedom, the flexibility of floating from vehicle to vehicle and from

issue to issue, which obviously leads to a multiparty. But I think that instead of a party in a structural sense, it's a party on a functional base. Look at the great issues now that, more and more, are being formulated by the environmental groups, consumer protection groups. . . . More influence today and more momentum and more activity is being generated by these functional groups on specific issues than by both political parties put together.

While Hatfield's functionalism offers the advantages of political diversity and freedom from party tradition, the system also has some drawbacks. For instance, functionalism might lead to oppression of other groups or nonaligned individuals. A functional system might limit political participation to those groups which accept certain short-term—possibly materialistic—goals. (Most groups are not likely to be as idealistic as, say, the Nader organization or Common Cause.) If that should happen, what recourse would be available to other groups, such as those organized around long-term, nonmaterialistic issues like ideology, ethnicity, or religion? Would poorer, ideologically oriented groups always be at a disadvantage against wealthier interest groups?

There may be several reasons why Hatfield suggests functionalism, rather than a complete multiparty approach, as the system of the future. First, to advocate a multiparty system would be risky for a politician whose power base, at present, is founded on one of the two major parties. Second, the senator has shown little sympathy for *public* political expression of religious, ethnic, or strong ideological opinions. Third, although Hatfield indicates an affinity for the British parliamentary system, he apparently has little substantial knowledge of the most successful multiparty parliamentary democracies—Switzerland and the Netherlands. Those countries have proved that a mature citizenry can handle the inevitable divisiveness of religious, ethnic, and ideological politics.[9]

In summary, structural reform of the political party system itself is one area where Mark Hatfield's reforms didn't keep pace with his frustrations. He remained somewhat a pragmatist, not so much proposing functionalism as making room for it in the context of a disintegrating two-party system.

The Beam in Our Eye

> Our first priority must be to restore our own society and to
> attend to its injustices before we presume to tell others how
> to set their houses in order. We cannot hope to transplant
> the American Dream on foreign soil before it has become
> firmly rooted in our own.[1]

ONCE THE 1973 PEACE accords halted America's direct military
action in Vietnam, Senator Hatfield was anxious to tackle matters of
global concern, particularly world hunger and poverty. But he
realized that nagging problems at home must be solved before
concerned leaders could kindle the interest of Americans in critical
issues abroad.

Perhaps the most pressing domestic question was whether to
grant amnesty to thousands of draft evaders and deserters of the
1960s and early '70s. Could the United States' middle-aged legislators and government executives—many of them veterans of earlier wars—forgive the angry young men of the Vietnam era? Not
without considerable soul-searching. Attitudes toward war had
been different a generation earlier. Hatfield himself had considered it a privilege to serve in World War II.

Predictably, many of those who fought with pride in World War
II or Korea considered the deserters, draft-card burners, and
conscientious objectors of the Vietnam era to be nothing more than
unpatriotic shirkers. Hatfield, however, because of the transformation in his own life, urged that the nation grant amnesty quickly: "I
think it's rather a moot point whether we let them back today or
whether we restore them to citizenship tomorrow. We're going to.
And I think it's far more honest to do it outright, head-on, than to

123

go through the charades of an amnesty program whereby you work your way back into good citizenship."

In the book *Amnesty? The Unsettled Question of Vietnam*,[2] Hatfield pointed out that amnesty or pardons had been granted to some degree after wars throughout U.S. history. For instance, after World War II, President Harry Truman created an amnesty board to consider the cases of some 15,000 violators of the Selective Service Act. (The board recommended amnesty for some of them; Truman pardoned all the violators a short time later.)

Hatfield observed in this book that the sentiment against amnesty

> stems from the deep desire to believe our nation has done no wrong. We want desperately to believe that our peace has brought honor. . . . The idea that we can achieve national "honor" out of this nightmare of moral agony is a threatening, dangerous illusion that must be decisively discarded. . . . We need a spirit of repentance in our land.

The senator suggested that Americans also needed to repent of the manner in which the war was conducted (i.e., through the arbitrary exercise of presidential power built upon the questionable foundation of military conscription). Continuing the spirit of his earlier opposition to the draft, Hatfield linked conscription to a larger issue in a plea for national forgiveness:

> In essence, conscription is a form of involuntary servitude. . . . *But we cannot try to defend freedom at home or create it abroad by taking it away from our own citizens—we cannot export what we do not have.* . . .
>
> We must recognize the severity of choices faced by young men who were morally opposed to the war. They had to reconcile their duty to country with their duty to conscience.
>
> The choices they faced often became desperate. They could attempt to achieve status as conscientious objectors to all war. . . . If this failed . . . they could choose to move to Canada or elsewhere, or to go to jail, or to kill men they did not hate in a war they could not justify for a cause they did not believe in.
>
> . . . I believe that the conscription . . . was an unjust in-

fringement upon the most fundamental rights of the citizen. Therefore, my disposition is to be generous, sympathetic, and comprehensive in granting amnesty to those who held similar convictions, but went to jail, left the country, or are culpable under the demands of the law in other ways for the sake of their beliefs.[3]

Hatfield recommended a radical program of *full amnesty* for all conscientious objectors as well as for draft evaders, draft resisters, and deserters whose protest did not endanger the lives or damage the property of others. He was distressed at the hostility expressed by the Nixon Administration toward amnesty. Later he even called it hypocrisy for a nation to pardon a president for known crimes while refusing to forgive young men who had declined, for reasons of conscience, to kill men they didn't even know.

In concluding his treatise on amnesty, Hatfield observed that "our nation's foremost need is the recovery of a relevant moral conscience.... This must begin by healing the wounds that have taken root within our own hearts, and the reconciling of ourselves to each other."[4] Only then could the proper elements of the American dream be offered to others.

In an effort to spark a spirit of repentance among Americans—a prerequisite to a new foreign policy, a new role in foreign affairs—Hatfield proposed that April 30, 1974, be observed as a "National Day for Humiliation, Fasting, and Prayer." The resolution was modeled after President Abraham Lincoln's Proclamation of a Day of Humiliation, Fasting, and Prayer exactly 111 years earlier—April 30, 1863, in the midst of the Civil War. As in Lincoln's proclamation, Hatfield's Senate resolution called for Americans to confess and repent of national sins. It was a message many Americans didn't want to hear, particularly at the conclusion of the United States' frustrating role in the Vietnam War:

> Whereas, it is the duty of nations, as well as of men to owe their dependence upon the overruling power of God, to confess their sins and transgressions, in humble sorrow, yet with assured hope that genuine repentance will lead to mercy and pardon, and to recognize the sublime truth, announced in the Holy Scriptures and proven by all history,

that those nations are blessed whose God is the Lord; and

Whereas, we know that we have been the recipients of the choicest bounties of Heaven; we have been preserved these many years in peace and prosperity; we have grown in numbers, wealth and power as no other nation has ever grown; but we have forgotten God; and

Whereas, we have forgotten the gracious hand which preserved us in peace, and multiplied and enriched us; and we have vainly imagined, in the deceitfulness of our hearts, that all these blessings were produced by some superior wisdom and virtue of our own; and

Whereas, intoxicated with unbroken success, we have become too self-sufficient to feel the necessity of redeeming and preserving grace, too proud to pray to the God that made us; and

Whereas, we have made such an idol out of our pursuit of "national security" that we have forgotten that only God can be the ultimate guardian of our true livelihood and safety; and

Whereas, we have failed to respond, personally and collectively, with sacrifice and uncompromised commitment to the unmet needs of our fellow man, both at home and abroad; as a people, we have become so absorbed with the selfish pursuits of pleasure and profit that we have blinded ourselves to God's standard of justice and righteousness for this society; and

Whereas, it therefore behooves us to humble ourselves before Almighty God, to confess our national sins, and to pray for clemency and forgiveness: Now, therefore be it

Resolved by the Senate and House of Representatives of the United States of America in Congress Assembled that the Congress hereby proclaims that April 30, 1974, be a National Day of Humiliation, Fasting and Prayer; and calls upon the people of our nation to humble ourselves as we see fit, before our Creator to acknowledge our final dependence upon Him and to repent of our national sins.[5]

That remarkable resolution passed the Senate by voice vote, perhaps due in part to the senators' eagerness to recess for the 1973

Christmas holidays. In the House, however, the bill bogged down in committee and was never approved. (Many individual Christian churches and denominations did follow Hatfield's suggestion and observed a day of humiliation, fasting, and prayer.)

Public reaction was mixed. Syndicated columnist Garry Wills (in the *Washington Star*, January 23, 1974) praised the resolution as being what America needed. Wills suggested that those of the political right needed such a day because of their inconsistency: they accepted corporate (i.e., national) accomplishments, but they wouldn't acknowledge corporate guilt. Art Buchwald satirized the proposal in a column which the *Los Angeles Times* (January 8, 1974) headlined "The Day We All Eat Humble Pie." The *Portland Oregonian* (January 14, 1974) editorially disapproved: "The editors believe this resolution, if passed, would be found to be unconstitutional because it proposes to use essentially religious means to serve governmental ends, where secular means would suffice." Arizona's Senator Goldwater, indicating that he had unlimited pride in America, said gratitude to God was one thing, "but if there is to be any suggestion in the resolution that we as a nation and people should feel humiliated, I cannot agree."[6] Never was the difference between persons like Goldwater and Hatfield more evident than in the Oregonian's remarks during the April 30, 1974, service at the National Presbyterian Church in the nation's capital:

> As the wealthiest nation on earth, we are inclined to use our power to satisfy our own national needs. As we become richer, the less affluent nations of the world, from which we extract our national resources, become increasingly poorer. The exploitation of the poor countries, even though not totally without benefit for those countries, is demanded by the consumption of products they do not enjoy. . . .
>
> In theological terms we can view this consumptive-disposability-convenience mindset as a lack of stewardship. The book of *Genesis* tells us that God created the world, and it was good. Man was given the job as the caretaker of Creation. However, we have failed miserably in that task. . . . In our own desire for material goods, we have polluted our sky and waterways, creating an ecological imbal-

ance that threatens the life of our planet . . . we must begin
to understand that we are a part of the Creation ourselves,
and to do injustice to the earth in search of material wealth is
to destroy a part of ourselves and does offense to the
Creator.[7]

Hatfield was uncomfortable with the entire framework within
which American foreign policy functioned in the early and mid-
'70s. He wanted America to abandon its self-asserted role as the
world's policeman and instead play the role of peacemaker and
"good neighbor" to those in need. The lesson of Vietnam, he feels,
was that "a foreign policy cannot be undertaken and promulgated
that is exercised only through force. Short of an all-out war, a
unilateral military action to execute a foreign policy is sheer stupid-
ity." Not only does a military-oriented foreign policy cost many
lives, it also devours an inordinate portion of the gross national
product and the energy of the people. In his eyes, that is a lesson
we should have learned from earlier wars.

Since World War II, America's foreign policy had been based
upon *realism*—which was rooted in "amorality" rather than in a
sense of moral responsibility. According to Hatfield, the
superstructure of that amoral foreign policy was supported by
three shaky pillars: (1) anticommunism, (2) military extravagance,
and (3) national self-interest. Of special importance was the de-
bilitating effect of self-centered nationalism, which had, for example, undermined U.S. objectives in Indochina:

A calculus of our own national interests, devoid of basic
moral concerns, has consistently been at the heart of our
[Vietnam] intervention.

. . . we have based our policy on the exclusive pursuit of
our self interest rather than adhering to fundamental moral
claims and considerations.[8]

Such a *realistic* foreign policy left no room for humanistic issues
like world hunger, Hatfield maintained. So concerned was
America with manipulating the economies of other nations and
repelling the Communist menace, he said, that problems such as
hunger didn't figure into the diplomatic "calculus." Because of that
realistic bias, America was in danger of losing her national integrity.

There was another problem. Hatfield believed that Third World peoples were becoming aware of what was happening around them. Since America supported the "Establishment" in these countries, natives looked upon the United States as a counter-revolutionary force slowing their move toward social and economic justice. The "battle" against communism could be won only if the United States hammered out a new foreign policy based on the "unity and commonality of mankind". We can win the battle, he said, "if we bind up their wounds, if we show them how to grow enough food, if we educate their children, and if we love them."[9]

This positive approach to foreign policy stands in stark contrast to America's practice during the past three decades. Hatfield was convinced that such a transformation was necessary if America was to assume its proper place of (moral) leadership among the nations of the world.

Hatfield also rejected the typical American diplomatic principle of supporting "puppet regimes" throughout the world. He suggested instead a policy which would uphold the dignity and value of individual human beings (the image-bearers of God). This approach, rooted in the spiritual resources of the Judeo-Christian tradition, would enhance family units and small, communal life-styles. A return to civil religion? No. His suggestion reflects consistent biblical insight and a remarkable capacity for Christian love. Explains former Senator Harold Hughes, a Democrat from Iowa and Hatfield's closest friend in the Senate: "Christ is so much in the center of Hatfield's life that he couldn't make a decision without it having an effect. I don't think you can separate the man from his Christ."

Hatfield's Christ-centered idealism drove him to reject the conventional realistic belief that American foreign policy could function amorally. No one and no government can function in a moral vacuum, he declared. Either one functioned morally (in tune with a higher moral law) or immorally (out of tune with that law)—but never amorally. Realists (like many Vietnam defenders) who hid behind a mask of amoral neutrality actually espoused immoral principles. It was time for a fresh approach:

> Realists have ruled the world for decades. Who is satisfied by the results? We can do no worse, now, than to respond to

man's ideals, to moral demands, and to the dictates of compassion. Indeed, only such a response can begin to open
man's hope for the future.[10]

Hatfield's appeal to idealism represents a considerable evolution
from his early political years, when, he says, he "would have been
the imperialist of imperialists." He attributes this change to a
growing sensitivity to

other kinds of imperialism—economic imperialism, cultural
imperialism. And that imperialism is inherently, basically,
ultimately, initially, and throughout exploitative. And it's
exploitative of other than tea and rubber and resources. It's
basically exploitative of people because in the quest for tea
and rubber, people are expendable. All you're motivated by
is markets. . . .

To Mark Hatfield, people are not expendable. U.S. foreign
policy must be based on something more important than preserving markets for American corporations!

Blessed, and Hungry,
Are the Poor

> It is easy enough to tell the poor to accept their poverty as
> God's will when you yourself have warm clothes and plenty
> of food and medical care and a roof over your head and no
> worry about the rent. But if you want them to believe
> you—try to share some of their poverty and see if you can
> accept it as God's will yourself!
>
> Thomas Merton[1]

NOWHERE ARE THE poor hungrier, the ill more distressed,
than in Calcutta, India's city of palaces and slums. There, one of
God's choice servants, Mother Teresa, pours out unparalleled
Christian compassion upon the neediest of the unfortunate millions. Her Roman Catholic Sisters of Charity are not confined by
convent walls; they minister in the streets.

One day in March 1974 Senator and Mrs. Hatfield and their two
older children followed that "living saint of God" on her rounds
through the byways of Calcutta. They saw Mother Teresa pick up
the dying and take them to a shelter. She bathed them, fed them,
loved them, so that they could die with dignity. That experience
was etched deeply into the senator's heart.

Speaking at a Western Conservative Baptist Seminary dinner
just three weeks later, Hatfield said of Mother Teresa:

> I went with her to the leper area where the vultures sit up on
> the bridge waiting for someone to die, people with no fin-
> gers, no hands, no nose, no feet. Mother Teresa moved
> among these people, taking them by the shoulder and
> steadying them, touching their arms, loving them. The
> babies that are left and abandoned she takes in to feed. . . . As
> we drove down a street and saw a body that had just died

131

only a few minutes before, still lying there waiting to be removed like garbage; and as we walked through rows of cots where the elderly were there perspiring on the brow, because maybe in an hour or two they would pass on, Mother Teresa said to me: "Before every single person dies we tell them about Jesus."

Mother Teresa told Hatfield about a memorable time when she took rice to a family that hadn't eaten for three days. As she doled out the rice, Mother Teresa noticed the mother putting part of the rice into another container. Why? "The mother replied that there was a neighbor family which had not eaten for three days either. She wanted to share her rice with them. 'I could have given a double portion of rice,' Mother Teresa told us, 'but I did not want to deny this family the blessing of sharing.'"[2]

That "blessing of sharing" reminded Hatfield of his first glimpses of real hunger nearly three decades earlier. In September 1945, just a month after American atomic bombs had devastated the Japanese cities of Hiroshima and Nagasaki, Lieutenant Hatfield and several Navy colleagues viewed the destruction. Memories of Iwo Jima and Okinawa were strong in the Americans' minds; they hated the enemy. Traveling in small landing craft, they docked at Hiroshima. Once ashore, the Navy men "saw immediately the scarcity of food among the Japanese. Most were drawn to give their lunches to the frightened, hungry children of Hiroshima. Suddenly we were sharing food with people who had been our archenemies a few weeks before."[3]

Little more than a month later, Hatfield's ship steamed to the Indochina port of Haiphong to pick up Nationalist Chinese troops and ferry them to battle with the Chinese Communists in Manchuria. Shortly after the ship anchored at Haiphong, it was surrounded by hungry Vietnamese in fishing boats, begging for food. When the Navy cooks dumped garbage overboard, the natives rescued every scrap. Hatfield was among the officers going ashore to get the Chinese troops:

I remember as we were going along the road from Haiphong to Hanoi that there were bodies of dead people along the road. Dead not by war or by bullets, but dead because of starvation. Babies, young people, old people—people dead, bloated, starved to death. And that indelible impression will never be erased from my mind. . . .

And the starvation that existed there was of such magnitude it impressed upon me that all the bullets and all the guns and all the propaganda would never change a person's mind who had but one thought . . . each day—to find enough food to stay alive for that day before he went to bed.[4]

Memories of Haiphong and Calcutta have convinced Hatfield that solutions to world hunger must incorporate both spiritual and physical dimensions—a biblically holistic approach. Political remedies are not sufficient in themselves. By the time foreign aid trickles through many hands in other governments, he told the Baptist seminarians, "there is very little left" for the people who are starving. Christians, however, apart from what governments may or may not do, must be ready with compassion for body and soul:

How dare we offer Christ as the Bread of Life to a hungry man when we have no compassion to find the bread to feed his stomach! I say to you, this world . . . is in need of . . . the message of redemption *and* the mission of compassion and service. Part of our repentance can be accomplished through the physical, external act of supplying the world's food needs. But that is not enough. It must be joined and nurtured by a spiritual, internal act of prayer under the leadership of the Holy Spirit.[5]

The related issues of hunger and poverty compelled Hatfield to spell out the implications—for Christians and America—of his approach to foreign policy and international relations. As he began to concentrate on the complexities of world hunger, he realized how insufficient political remedies are by themselves. Nowhere was this made clearer than at Rome during the World Food Conference in November 1974. As one of the U.S. delegates to the conference, he listened as representatives of the United Nations (the sponsoring organization) and Third World countries recited the problems:

—With the world's population (about 4 billion) increasing by 2 percent annually, it will take only thirty-five years for that population to double. Demand for food will grow even faster.

—Global weather problems in 1972 decreased total food production for the first time in two decades, shrinking the world's food-grain stores to a twenty-seven-day supply. The result? Sharply higher prices. Every increase in food prices seals the fate of more hungry residents of underdeveloped nations; they are priced out of the food market—and life itself.

—The heralded "Green Revolution," while successful in developing higher-yielding varieties of key grains such as wheat and rice, had drawbacks, too. To capitalize on the new varieties, farmers needed enormous quantities of fertilizer and water. Huge quantities of energy are needed to produce fertilizer; with energy prices soaring, even farmers in affluent nations could scarcely afford enough fertilizer.

—If Third World countries adopted farming techniques based on the Green Revolution and U.S. big business practices, they would need huge investments in machines. That would cause more problems, a delegate from Tanzania wisely observed to Hatfield: "How foolish for some of these developing countries to be talking about capital intensive investment. In my country, if we had a tractor there would be one man running that tractor and 1,000 men watching him. We need *labor* intensive development."[6]

—Probably half a *billion* people in the world faced starvation or malnutrition within eight months from the end of the Rome conference.

—Half of the deaths of children in the world are in one way or another attributable to malnutrition. The immediate effect of malnutrition is obvious. Yet the long-term effect might be greater, for malnutrition in the early years can result in permanent brain damage.

Alarmed by such reports, Hatfield immediately proposed massive U.S. food exports to alleviate the short-term crisis. And true to his radical image he suggested long-term assistance through changes in the American lifestyle, rather than through the conventional means—like selling bigger tractors to the poor. For instance, he suggested that reducing U.S. meat consumption by 5 percent would free 6 million tons of grain for direct consumption by the hungry elsewhere. By redirecting food exports from affluent countries, the senator said, more of the needy could be fed. He was stunned by the response of the U.S. secretary of agriculture, Earl Butz, who headed the American delegation in Rome. Butz, Hatfield related,

> attempted to dismiss the issue by stating that when the Conference was planned last spring, its purpose was to deal with long-range questions. But the grim, desperate plight faced by the world's multitudes this November was not foreseen last spring. . . . Contending that the World Food Conference should not have focused unduly on those who are now dying from hunger is like urging firemen to ignore blazing cities in favor of discussions about future fire prevention.
>
> Nero fiddled while Rome burned; at the Food Conference, our government fiddled while the world starved. Our eventual decision not to modestly increase our food aid to the world's hungry deepened the pangs of conscience among millions of Americans while worsening the pangs of hunger across the globe. . . .[7]

America's official response to the food crisis was particularly galling to Hatfield because he knew what this country was capable of doing. During the early part of World War I, Herbert Hoover headed the Commission for Relief in Belgium, and after the war he directed all relief and rehabilitation efforts for the Allied powers. His organizations fed millions of starving Europeans, mostly via private donations and government appropriations from the United States. When the United States entered the war in 1917, President Woodrow Wilson named Hoover the U.S. food administrator and charged him with mobilizing food resources for the Allied cause.

Hoover encouraged Americans to reduce domestic consumption and eliminate waste. The results, Hatfield pointed out, were incredible. That first year the United States increased food exports by 5.4 million tons, to a total of 12.4 million tons. "And in 1918, when we had been able to institute increased food production, we increased the exports to 18 million tons; the goal of 20 million tons

of export was achieved in 1919. Mr. Hoover said this was accomplished primarily through the giving of the American
people."[8]

If Americans were willing to sacrifice 60 years ago, wouldn't they
do so again—if they knew their efforts would aid the hungry? Butz
told delegates in Rome that the United States had as much as 5.5
million tons of available surpluses, worth $1.4 to 1.5 billion. That
much food was available even without sacrifices; yet President
Gerald Ford's budget trimmed that figure by some 25 percent.

When Hatfield returned from Rome, he introduced a
"Thanksgiving Resolution" in the Senate to call attention to the
hunger problem. The resolution asked that Americans (1) observe
the time from Thanksgiving Day 1974 to Thanksgiving Day 1975 as
a year of identification with the hungry of the world; (2) designate
the Monday of Thanksgiving week in 1975 as a National Day of
Fasting; (3) encourage fasting on holidays and special religious
days; (4) seek to change their lifestyles in order to conserve food;
(5) share a portion of their savings—achieved through conservation
efforts—with the starving millions. To publicize his resolution, the
senator hosted a luncheon on Capitol Hill. The guests, including
congressmen and news reporters, dined on a "meal" consisting of
little more than a hard roll. A *Washington Post* reporter (Nov. 26,
1974) called the meal—intended to be typical of what a Third-
World resident might have—"one of the strangest luncheons seen
in the Capitol. . . ." Like Hatfield's resolution calling for a day of
humiliation and fasting, this Thanksgiving Resolution passed the
Senate but not the House. Nevertheless, some individuals and
churches complied with the spirit of the "Thanksgiving Year"
proposal.

A few months earlier Hatfield had turned to the Food for Peace
Program under Public Law 480 in hopes of increasing the official
U.S. response to the problem of global hunger. He soon discovered that PL480 hid more than it revealed about America's
"humanitarian" foreign aid. Food for Peace was thoroughly
politicized.

The law had two parts. Title I allowed concessional loans—not
gifts—to other countries for the value of the food. Title II, usually a

smaller figure, provided direct gifts of food to needy nations. Hatfield voiced two primary objections. First, the amount of food given away had declined steadily since the late 1960s. Then, the average was about 9 million tons of food annually. The 1974 figure—which President Gerald Ford's Administration refused to increase—was 4.3 million tons. Second, the senator found that most Title I grants were made to our allies in the Indochina war. Instead of buying food, the loans were being used to acquire arms to continue the fighting! In 1974 about the same amount—$190 million—of Title I grants went to Cambodia, with 7 million people, as to the whole continent of Africa, with a population of 550 million.

Speaking on the Senate floor (July 22, 1974), Hatfield charged that priorities "governing the Food for Peace Program are clear. They are to support economies geared to war, rather than relieve famine and starvation. Almost half of last year's Food for Peace allocations turned out, in fact, to be food for war." In addition, Title II gifts weren't limited to food. Frequently, other countries bought commodities such as tobacco and cotton—which they quickly sold at a profit to buy other products, including military supplies.

Hatfield suggested three simple and far-reaching reforms: (1) remove political considerations from the entire Food for Peace program; (2) grant aid, both loans and gifts, only to the truly needy countries; (3) remove nonfood products from the program. Early in 1975 Hatfield and other senators, particularly Hubert Humphrey of Minnesota, pushed restrictive legislation through Congress. The new law decreed that no more than 30 percent of Title I concessional aid could be used for political purposes rather than for countries designated as needy by the United Nations. Hatfield was somewhat disappointed with the 30 percent limitation, but the compromise was necessary to get the legislation passed. Similarly he wasn't able to reclassify tobacco and cotton into a new nonfood aid category under PL480.[9]

It wasn't long before the Ford Administration counterattacked. Neither the State Department (which was fond of aid for political purposes) nor the Agriculture Department (the proponent of food aid as a way to develop future markets) was happy with the restrictions. Hatfield was particularly upset when Secretary of State

Henry Kissinger sought to circumvent the 30 percent limit in his requests for more aid to South Vietnam, Chile, and Korea. These nations, Hatfield pointed out, clearly did not qualify for additional aid: "The Congress has expressed its will, and written a law. The task of the executive branch is to enforce that law, not circumvent or ignore it."[10] In spite of the new congressional restrictions, Hatfield realized that more radical legislation was needed to curb executive power and instill humanitarianism into American foreign aid.

A month after returning from the World Food Conference, he proposed the creation of a cabinet-level Office of Food Administration. The food administrator—patterned after Hoover's World War I position—would coordinate relief efforts. In February 1975 Hatfield put his proposal into legislative form. He suggested that the administrator be appointed by the president, confirmed by the Senate, and assigned the task of overcoming the bureaucratic inertia often typical of overlapping relief efforts.

"The food administrator I propose could put an end to this bureaucratic delay and exert the leadership to mobilize Americans in support of a coherent and humane food aid policy," the senator said.[11] All other agencies were directed to cooperate with the food administrator, who alone was responsible for relief recommendations to the president. It was one of the few instances when Hatfield urged centralized power. Because the proposal would undermine the entrenched authority of existing bureaucracies, it received little support in the Senate.

Despite Hatfield's dislike for the Vietnam War, he pressed hard for economic and humanitarian assistance for Indochina after direct American involvement ended early in 1973. Early in 1975, when the collapse of both South Vietnam and Cambodia was obvious, he urged a halt to military aid coupled with an accelerated program of humanitarian assistance. He sponsored a bill, which quickly passed in the Senate, providing that henceforth all military aid to Cambodia and South Vietnam be used instead for such humanitarian purposes as refugee relief. At the conclusion of U.S. involvement in Vietnam, Hatfield's compassion was clear:

The high expectations I sensed among the people of Vietnam in 1945 for establishing an independent nation may finally be realized after thirty years of violence and civil war which was so meaningless and futile.

The deep sense of relief that this war is finally at an end does not abrogate our responsibility to help rebuild a land and a people so utterly torn asunder.

If we courageously and honestly face the failure of our past policies, we may learn to correct our ways for the future.[12]

Hatfield didn't confine his post-Rome humanitarian work to the Senate chamber. As chairman of Project FAST ("Fight Against Starvation Today"), sponsored by World Vision International, he wrote a series of articles on hunger for Christian magazines. The themes—often the very words—were virtually identical: they spelled out Hatfield's vision of Christian economic stewardship in the world, along with some practical ways for Christians to help alleviate world hunger. These articles appeared in such magazines as *Eternity, The Lutheran Standard, Moody Monthly, Post American, Campus Life, Brother's Newsletter, The Other Side,* and *World Vision.*

In these articles the senator emphasized the gravity of the situation. "No problem is more likely to breed instability and conflict, and increase the magnitude of mankind's suffering in the years directly ahead, than the shortage of food," he wrote.[13]

What about the energy shortage? "The scarcity of energy worsens the shortage of food," he pointed out. "With the increasing mechanization of farming it takes about eighty gallons of gas to raise an acre of corn. . . . Thus, while Americans waited in line a few hours for gas for their cars, Indian farmers waited in line for five days for gas to run their irrigation pumps. . . ."[14]

Another problem, one about which man can do little, is climate. The senator noted that climatologists say the world's average temperature has dropped in recent decades, causing desert areas to expand toward the equator. (An example is found in the sub-Sahara region of Africa, where the expanding desert resulted in the starvation of hundreds of thousands.)

But is the real problem simply a lack of food? Are, in fact, the world's resources insufficient to feed its people? In reply, Hatfield was fond of quoting Mahatma Gandhi: "The earth provides enough for every man's need, but not for every man's greed."[15]

The senator emphasized that the greed of the Western world was the primary culprit. The affluent nations contain but one-third of the world's population, yet they consume two-thirds of the earth's protein resources. Americans, in particular, are to blame:

> Although Americans constitute only six percent of the world's population, we consume forty percent of the world's resources. . . . If our wasteful rate of consumption . . . is a bit abstract when we think in terms of automobiles, large electrical appliances, and heavy tanks, it becomes very practical when we consider American food consumption.
>
> While most of the world relies on cereals and vegetable protein to feed its hungry people, we gorge ourselves on red meat.[16]

The average American, he pointed out, consumed nearly a ton of grain annually in the mid-1970s. But an American consumed only 150 pounds of grain directly, in the form of breads and breakfast cereal. The other 1,850 pounds of grain come indirectly from meat, milk, and eggs. In many poor countries, per capita grain consumption is but 400 pounds a year; little or none of that can be spared for animals. "Thus," Hatfield wrote, "while much of the world is on the edge of starvation, consuming only 400 pounds of grain per year per person, we Americans use four times that amount to feed our cows, pigs, and chickens. . . . Our high rate of meat consumption is the main reason why it takes five times the agricultural resources of land, water, and fertilizer to support an American as it does to support an Indian, Nigerian, or Colombian."[17]

To narrow the gap between the poor and wealthy countries, the senator said, conventional answers—such as technological improvements—are not enough. High-yield crops, irrigation, mechanization, and fertilizer will not solve long-term problems if neither poor growers nor poor consumers can pay the extra cost.

What structural reforms are needed? "It is hard to envision successful development in the poor nations of the world if comprehensive land reform and income redistribution are not made the first tasks," the senator wrote.[18] Land reform did not mean creating huge, American-sized farms. He suggested family-sized units, large enough to support the tenants but small enough to do without the expensive, energy-guzzling mechanization of U.S. agriculture. Could such small units be productive enough to make an impact? While we think of U.S. farms as the ultimate in food production, Hatfield pointed out that intensive cultivation of small units in such countries as Japan and Taiwan yields more food per acre.

To finance these reforms, Hatfield suggested that cooperatives be formed. Outside assistance, whether in the form of education or grants, should be directed toward the cooperative organizations and the small farmers themselves. Such labor-intensive rural development would go a long way toward solving the unemployment problem mentioned by the Tanzanian delegate at the conference in Rome.

Hatfield admits there are significant obstacles to his land-reform program. First, much of the land to be reallocated now belongs to rich land barons and multinational corporations. Short of revolution, how can this land be distributed in family-sized units? Leaders of these poor nations may be among the landholders; reform would threaten their own power bases.

Even radical land reform would not be the entire solution. "Famine cannot be averted by simply thinking we can increase the 'size of the pie,' so those who have little may have a little more," Hatfield asserted. "What we are discovering is that the pie itself has limits."[19] There aren't enough beefsteaks for everyone in our global village. To insure that Mother Teresa has rice for Calcutta's hungry, he suggested a lifestyle tempered by compassion and a spirit of repentance: "All of us, as a nation, have a responsibility to feed the hungry of the world. Each of us, as consumer, participates in a lifestyle that robs the poor of all but a few crumbs so that we ... can feast. As Christians, all of us—and each of us—must repent."[20] Hatfield predicted that such a transformation would be particularly difficult for Americans, who have suffered relatively little from the ravages of disease and war.

How can Christians help? Hatfield suggested that individuals as well as churches support the organized relief agencies, both secular and Christian—with our skills as well as our money. In addition, we could renew the practice of fasting periodically (and give money saved to relief groups), we could minimize waste, limit consumption of meat, plant home gardens, feed scraps instead of commercial food to pets, and conserve all the earth's resources.

Readers of the magazines didn't all rush to the aid of the needy. Many found Hatfield's suggestions discomforting. Letters to *Moody Monthly* (March and April, 1975) are indicative of the response:

> I'm crazy about *Moody Monthly*, but I object to nausea by liberals like Mark Hatfield. Mr. Hatfield . . . would do well to extol the Christian virtue of hard work and individual initiative rather than lecture Conservative Baptists on their greed. . . . It's the same old socialist blah and it's sickening. . . .
>
> Our first charge from the Lord Jesus is to preach the Gospel. There is no other command to feed the world. You know according to God's word we will have the poor with us always. . . .
>
> . . . so the good old U. S. A. should again come to the rescue of the world as we have been doing for years. This time send not only excess crops to the hungry nations but take food off our tables to send to them. . . . Are we biblically to feed an enemy nation, Mr. Hatfield? No, we are not.

The senator rejected outright suggestions that "it is God's will" that some be hungry. In reply, he quotes Dr. Vernon Grounds, longtime president of the Conservative Baptist Theological Seminary in Denver: "We may believe that history will end in utter destruction before the New Jerusalem comes into being. But that should not deter us from ministering to the world's suffering and need any more than the knowledge of the eventual death of every person would lead us to abandon any ministry to sickness and disease."[21]

Hatfield's stance on world hunger and poverty is a good example of his unconventional political wisdom. Philosophical conservatives—including many evangelicals—pin their solution to hunger on the dynamics of the free market. They seek to export capital-intensive technology and bolster the market potential of Third World countries. Modern liberals, on the other hand, are more inclined simply to give aid to distressed nations—a commendable short-term goal, but one that can lead to serious problems when applied as a long-term solution. It can encourage the self-righteous feeling of paternalism at home and make needy nations overdependent upon the United States at a time when their serious internal problems need to be addressed. And in neither case do individual Americans seriously consider significant changes in their own lifestyles.

The senator's "politics of compassion" can largely be attributed to the interrelated forces of radical Anabaptism and neo-Hooverism. Sadly, this has led him into confrontation with conservative evangelicals and has contributed to his political isolation. His legislative proposals have gotten some support and progressive evangelicals are sympathetic, but his overall vision and program are too unconventional, too idealistic, to gather massive support.

The senator's dismay at official U.S. insensitivity to world hunger and his distress at evangelical apathy, however, contributed to his eagerness to outline his perspective. This led to his masterpiece, *Between a Rock and a Hard Place*, which was published in 1976.

Vintage Hatfield

> Most members of Congress try to pride themselves as being
> "influential". . . . they attempt to take credit for any govern-
> ment project announced in their state or district whether
> they had any influence over it or not. . . .
>
> A facade of statesmanlike idealism conceals a brothel of
> egomania and lust for power which prostitute those in politi-
> cal life for often nothing more than personal vainglory.
>
> I was sick and tired of this. . . .[1]

DR. CARL F. H. HENRY called *Between a Rock and a Hard Place*
"a forthright book that will gratify some readers, dismay others, but
challenge all. . . . Hatfield reaches with deep evangelical concern
for biblical authenticity in facing sociopolitical problems. . . . The
volume is refreshingly honest, its respect for Scripture unmistaka-
ble, and its desire to stand on biblical terrain under the lordship of
Christ highly commendable."[2]

James W. Skillen described the senator's book as "one of the
most unusual pieces of political literature in American history. I
know of no American politician who has gone back to the Bible with
such intensity and seriousness in quest of Christian foundations for
political service. . . . The Oregon Senator does not simply use God
and a few biblical quotations . . . he struggles from beginning to end
to understand the full scope of biblical revelation in its bearing on
human politics."[3]

Robert G. Clouse, after noting that "Hatfield's ability to identify
difficulties is not matched . . . by his proposed solutions," nevertheless said "the message is there. Evangelicals must match their
deeds with their words. . . . We must feed the hungry, clothe the

naked, and free victims of oppression. It is encouraging to know that there are believers like Senator Hatfield deeply involved in our nation's affairs who will remind Christians of their social duties."[4]

Prominent evangelical magazines called *Between a Rock and a Hard Place* one of the most significant books of the year. In several polls it placed second only to *Born Again*, by ex-Watergate conspirator Charles Colson.

The book summarizes the facets of Hatfield's spiritual and political thought. The imprint of general and neo-evangelicalism can be seen, as can that of Reformed Christianity. But the dominant force continues to be radical Anabaptism. For example, the book clearly reflects sympathy for the philosophical framework of *Sojourners* magazine. It was, in fact, a joint effort (under Hatfield's direction) between the senator and his former executive assistant, Wesley Michaelson. Michaelson, later associate editor of *Sojourners*, has been described by Hatfield as "an alter ego."

Perhaps the most vital message presented in the book concerns what Skillen referred to as "Christian foundations for political service." And the key is "service." Hatfield and Senator Harold Hughes labored over the question of how a disciple of Christ should function in politics. Writes Hatfield:

> Together we spent time struggling with these issues. Such discussion continued through the next two years, when Hughes decided not to run for reelection.
>
> My whole understanding of leadership and power underwent a fundamental change as I searched out my future.
>
> Power and prestige could not be the goals. . . . No longer could I define leadership in terms of holding positions of power. . . . Service to others, solely for their own behalf and even entailing deep sacrifice, is the true essence of leadership and the ultimate form of power.[5]

Who is the example for political leadership via "service to others"? As in earlier years, the senator can find only one answer—Jesus of Nazareth. In Luke 22:24-27 Jesus' disciples argued about which of them ranked highest. The Master set them straight: "The kings of the Gentiles exercise lordship over them. . . . But not so with you; rather let the greatest among you become as the youngest, and the leader as one who serves. . . . I am among you as one who serves."[6]

Jesus eloquently demonstrated his commitment to service by wrapping a towel around his waist, kneeling on the floor, and washing the feet of his disciples. Would any contemporary political leader—whether a city councilman in Bend, Oregon, or the president of the United States—perform a similar demeaning task for his constituents? Not in Hatfield's view. He believes American politicians are in love with their own positions of power, preferring to have their egos massaged by the trappings of political office.

Hatfield acknowledges that individual politicians cannot shoulder all the blame; the people, too, are guilty. In recent years the senator has spoken out against the tendency to look to Washington, especially the president, to solve our problems. Hatfield has called this situation America's "idolatrous" relationship to political power, for politicians and political answers are only part of the solution.

The model of Jesus suggests that political leadership is, in reality, political *service* and thus is a ministry for Christians who have the appropriate "calling." If a Christian politician is serious about fulfilling the servant-leader role, he is not obsessed with personal popularity and holding office. Rather, his key motive becomes

> the service of human need, and prophetic faithfulness to a vision of God's will being done "on earth as it is in heaven."
>
> Radical allegiance to Jesus Christ transforms one's entire perspective on political reality. . . . There is an uncompromised identification with the needs of the poor and the oppressed. . . . We are to empty ourselves as He did for the sake of others.[7]

That doesn't sound like the spirit of U.S. congressmen!

The typical political representative, Hatfield continues, is frequently insensitive to human suffering and not a likely candidate to "empty himself" for the sake of his constituents. He lashes out at the Senate—audaciously calling it a "brothel of egomania"—for creating "a facade of artificial cordiality, cloaking true feelings, and inhibiting close relationships."[8] If political leaders were committed to fulfilling the needs of "the poor and the oppressed" the power of love would be far more evident. But since political power is organized around materialistic values, Hatfield asserts that institutions

> become less capable of working for the needs of the poor and oppressed. Thus, our political structures and institutions fall under God's judgment; they are in rebellion, afflicted by the Fall, reflecting corporately the sin that lies within the hearts of men and women.[9]

Hatfield believes that a lost vision of justice is a basic weakness of the American political system. He realizes that institutions can, and often do, provide some good, but cautions Christians not to count on gradual structural reform of the "system" as a means of meeting human need. His neighborhood government plan (chapter ten) might facilitate a spiritual rebirth, but even a return to localism is no guarantee of such renewal.

Hatfield's radical Anabaptist perspective is further evident when considering his biblical concepts of the state and of early church-state relationships. For the senator, the Old Testament state was basically a negative institution, seldom fulfilling its office. The Israelite state, he maintains, usually sought to enhance its own power and frequently ended up on the side of the oppressor rather than the oppressed. In addition, those who seek to create a direct link between modern America and Old Testament Israel are off base: "Believing that our nation has a special dispensation of God's blessing as opposed, for instance, to Norway or Tanzania or Yugoslavia, simply confuses any biblical understanding of God's relationship to our nation and the world. God is not choosing special peoples over others in the modern world. . . ."[10] The senator does see an indirect link of accountability, however, between modern states and ancient Israel; even modern secular states remain under God's judgment.

It is the prophets of the Old Testament, not the kings, who draw most of Hatfield's attention. He praises the prophets for their courageous exposure of the pretentiousness and poor administration of justice on the part of the political establishment of their day.

They called for proper stewardship of natural resources and denounced economic injustice. In Hatfield's view, Christians today
should model their political stance after the Old Testament
prophets and call the establishment and the nation to repentance.
While the warnings of the prophets sometimes resulted in political
reform, he notes that the prophetic Word had "a life and a power of
its own, it did not need to be allied with the destiny of Israel's
political institutions. . . . God's Word today to the nations of the
world . . . possesses the same kind of relevance as did the prophetic
Word of the Old Testament."[11]

The senator's understanding of the New Testament concept of
the state is also fairly negative. At best, the state is a necessary evil.
Hatfield indicates strong similarities, however, between contemporary America and the people of Israel at the time of Christ:

> The outset of this decade in America was marked with draft
> resistance, massive protests against war . . . and strong dis-
> sent. . . . Still, most Christians were reluctant to believe that
> Jesus Christ had any concrete relevance to such issues, even
> though they knew Christ as their inward personal Savior.
> Yet they had not grasped the truth that his life was lived, like
> ours, amidst social upheaval, and that he was deeply in-
> volved in the struggles of his society. . . .
>
> In the context of his own time, Christ could only have
> been considered an opponent and a threat to the existing
> political and religious establishment. So it was that the Sad-
> ducees, the Pharisees, and the Roman officials together all
> conspired to put him to death.[12]

Indeed, even when Jesus was but an infant, King Herod considered the baby a threat to his political establishment. Later the
Pharisees confronted Jesus with the question of whether the Jews
should pay taxes to Caesar; Hatfield interprets Jesus' response this
way: ". . . there is a legitimate obligation which government can ask
of its citizens, but one with its boundaries sharply circum-
scribed. . . . Our heresy today comes in believing that the spheres
of Caesar and God are equal. . . . The coin, bearing Caesar's image . . . should be rendered to him. But the person, bearing the
image of God . . . should be given over wholly to his Service."[13]

Hatfield is most sympathetic with the radical Anabaptist theology of fallen worldly powers—which include "all those ideologies, forces, structures, and institutions that lie at the groundwork of a society or a culture, giving a sense of corporate cohesion."[14] The senator concedes a positive role for such powers ("they keep people alive and ordered in society").[15] But he seems to consider even that function little more than a necessary reality, insuring that the church can carry out its work.

What about the thirteenth chapter of Romans? Isn't Paul saying that everyone must submit to the "higher powers?" When considered in context—which extends from Romans 12:17 through Romans 13:10—Hatfield contends Paul's real message is that a Christian has *limited* allegiance to the state. He believes that the two keys to this passage are (1) that love overcomes vengeance, and (2) the notion of obedience or subjection really connotes a reciprocal obligation, a two-way responsibility. He holds that the perspective of unconditional acceptance of governmental authority "is that such a perspective is not sufficiently grounded in Scripture. . . . It is hard to believe that the government of Hitler's Nazi Germany, for instance, was divinely instituted and mandated, or that the same holds true for the autocracy of the Soviet Union. . . . the Christian must always view government as part of a fallen order and as motivated by its own pretensions and striving for power."[16] He warns Christians to be alert to the demonic potential of the state, which makes it an easy prey for Satan's forces.

How then should believers respond to government? Hatfield suggests five principles: (1) pray for the leaders of government; (2) respect those in authority; (3) obey civil laws, so long as they don't require Christians to disobey Christ; (4) pay taxes—although whether "specific portions of tax might be withheld . . . for activities which the Christian cannot condone could still be an open question";[17] (5) witness to government with prophetic power.

Hatfield traces the church's alliance with the political establishment back to the conversion of Constantine in the fourth century. Until that time, Christians and civil government were in constant conflict. For example, many Christians—though they faithfully paid their taxes—refused induction into the Roman army, declined to serve on juries in the court system, and would not swear an oath of allegiance to the Roman emperor. The senator says the early Christians' nonparticipation was founded on an ethic of love which forbade violence or support for any institution which encouraged violence.

After Constantine's conversion, however, the "Christian" empire graciously offered the church three privileges: (1) clergy would be exempt from taxes and military duty; (2) the church could have its own court system; (3) the church could own and receive property. As a result, church leaders felt obligated to support the political establishment's ever-expanding secular ventures. In Hatfield's view, *everything* changed as a result of the emperor's conversion: "The consequences . . . shaped the Church's attitude toward the State for the next fifteen hundred years, building up a legacy which has been with us to the present, distorting Christians' understanding of Scripture even in our own time."[18]

An important change, in the senator's assessment, was the perspective of many Christians toward violence. Before long, Christians began serving in the Roman army to help preserve a Christian empire against pagans. And by the fifth century, he says, *only* Christians could serve in the army. Ever since, Christians have become increasingly prone to violence—and to support institutions, such as the state, which are founded on violence.

Perhaps the most convincing evidence, then, of Hatfield's radical Anabaptism is his growing sympathy for pacifism. Earlier in life he had accepted the "just war" theory without qualms:

> Like most of my peers, I grew up in a time when the high-minded and utopian dreams of pacifism for the world were shattered by Hitler's *Blitzkrieg*. . . . I fought in the Pacific against the Japanese. . . . It was all a duty which seemed morally necessary. . . . But war itself? At the time, it was a necessary, though abhorrent, evil; we felt a patriotic duty to serve, and even a clear sense of righteous mission.[19]

However, his memorable experience at Hiroshima at the conclusion of World War II planted a question in his mind: Could there ever be virtue in war? Not until the escalation of America's involvement in Vietnam did that question come to the forefront. On the basis of his maturing theology, he finds no biblical evidence supporting an ethic of violence.

In the senator's view, proponents of just wars misinterpret Scripture, particularly Jesus' teaching in the Sermon on the Mount (the book of Matthew, chapters five through seven): "Christ's teaching about the forsaking of revenge and violence, and replacing it with love for one's enemies, is without qualification. Living under this mandate, how can we maim or injure anyone, and how can we take part in war and kill others?"[20] To Hatfield, then, love is without qualification: "In the death and resurrection of Christ, we see that God's love has the last word. That love was never compromised; evil was never returned by evil, but with a compassion grounded in the Father's love."[21] With love as an absolute standard for Christian conduct, violence or killing can never be justified.

The senator even extends this supposition to the Old Testament. His unconventional evangelical perspective is that the God of the Old Testament was a God who despised war. If that is true, why did the Israelites so often war against their neighbors? One important viewpoint, Hatfield says,

> asserts that a lack of trust and faithfulness on the part of the people of Israel, rather than the clear directive of God, brought them into warfare. . . .
>
> War was seen in the Old Testament as a means of judgment on a particular people. At times, the Israelites themselves came under the judgment of God for their unfaithfulness, and other peoples made war against them. In other cases, the people of Israel carried out God's judgment in their wars against others [22]

Opponents of nonviolence charge that such an approach is impractical, an evasion of moral responsibility. Not so, responds Hatfield; our moral duty is simply faithfulness to the Lord. Accordingly, a moral lifestyle means loving service to God and neighbor. It has nothing to do with violence.

Hence, evangelicals seeking to live by an ethic of love have two options—the "purist" and the "apologist" approach. The purist accepts the state as a necessary evil, granting that it will use violence, if necessary, to insure its own preservation. But the purist will have very little, if anything, to do with such an institution, he himself living by the principles of nonviolence. Even though that position might lead to withdrawal from the problems of the world, Hatfield says the purist should be commended because

> violence only begets violence, in a never-ending circle. By trusting in violence, we sow the seeds of our own destruction, as well as that of others. Humanity's hope lies with those who, possessed with faith and compassion, break that circle by demonstrating that evil is overcome by love.[23]

The senator, while praising the Christian apologist for wanting his faith to be relevant to modern society, sees a basic shortcoming: the apologist divides life into personal and national categories and limits the love command to the personal realm. The apologist accepts a personal ethic of love, but he doesn't believe it can be applied to society at large or to nations. Writes Hatfield: "According to the Apologist, I can personally love my enemies, including the Russians and the Chinese; but corporately, I must uphold the balance of power and arms in the absence of any trustworthy alternative."[24]

Apologists, the senator says, defend the "just war" theory by applying discriminating standards to test whether war may be justified: (1) the nation must realize that war is always terrible; (2) the war must be motivated by, and tempered with, a genuine caring for humanity; (3) the means must be consistent with the ends; (4) war must be the last resort; (5) war must be a defensive measure. Even considering these standards, Hatfield says "few if any of the wars we have fought meet all the requirements of a just war. Some, such as our intervention in Indochina, fail totally. Others, including World War II, were fought for better ends, yet with disproportionate means...."[25]

His most serious reservation about the apologist view is that "just war" can be an excuse for violent revolutions throughout the world—especially in underdeveloped nations:

> When a political regime of a poor nation is dictatorial,
> ruthlessly oppressive . . . and offers no hope to the poor mas-
> ses, then is not revolution committed to building justice for
> all a viable alternative?
>
> . . . When a fellow Christian from a poor nation tells me
> that violent revolution is the only option for freeing that
> country's masses from . . . suffering, then I find the just-war
> stance set forth in its most compelling manner.[26]

In spite of his sympathy for the oppressed, Hatfield cannot
condone violent revolution no matter how honorable the inten-
tions. The root of the problem is hatred—whether in the heart of
the revolutionary or the oppressor: "Violence and war are the
outgrowth of fears and hatreds. We fear those who threaten our
economic security; nations are vengeful toward those who
humiliate them; revolutionaries hate those who oppress them. The
result is an impulse to violence. Once these violent motives take
root, we search for means of justifying them."[27]

In principle, apologists condone violence only when motivated
by love. In practice, Hatfield believes this theory becomes the
rationalization for hate. He rejects the apologist's version of just
wars because the ends do not justify the means.

Of the two options, Hatfield clearly favors the purist position.
However, he suggests that some synthesis of the purist and
apologist options might be acceptable if the overall stance is one of
love. Is that a pacifistic viewpoint? Very close to it . . . but Hatfield
favors the term "nonviolence":

> The term "pacifism" [is] a word that denotes many things to
> many people. Pacifism, therefore, can become a code word
> which does not carry a very clear meaning. I would prefer to
> say that I have, in the last number of years, moved toward a
> position of trying to interpret Christian nonviolence. And I
> say "Christian nonviolence" because I find it increasingly
> difficult to reconcile the teachings of Christ to participating
> in any action of violence—whether under the aegis of the
> state or in personal relationships.
>
> I'm wrestling with the question. I haven't come down on
> all fours—but perhaps on three of the four points of landing
> on the [pacifist] side.

Quo Vadis?

> Perhaps I will only be a sower in terms of concepts or
> changes or reforms. Maybe the lot will fall to someone else to
> be the reaper, the harvester.... What I do must be in the
> context of redeeming the time and using the position I'm in
> to be faithful to God.[1]

ONE JANUARY NIGHT in 1973, Sen. John Stennis, the venerable Democrat from Mississippi, motored from Capitol Hill to his northwest Washington home. It was 7:40 p.m. when Stennis, 71, the powerful chairman of the Senate Armed Services Committee, parked the car and walked toward his house 50 feet away.

In the darkness two young robbers—little more than kids, really—confronted the senator. One held a .22-caliber pistol while the other relieved Stennis of his wallet, a gold wristwatch, his Phi Beta Kappa key, and a 25-cent piece. Stennis didn't fight, but—the attackers related later—he "started hollering and carrying on." Maybe the noise unnerved them, or maybe they were disgusted with the meager take in the robbery. "Now we're going to shoot you anyway," one told the senator.[2]

The young man with the pistol fired twice. One bullet tore through the senator's stomach, rupturing the pancreas and damaging the intestinal tract. The second bullet struck the senator's left thigh. Then the assailants fled.

Despite the wounds, Stennis struggled to his house for help. An ambulance sped him to Walter Reed Army Medical Center where surgeons labored for six-and-one-half hours to repair the damage and save his life. The senator's condition was critical.

Meanwhile, Senator Hatfield, driving home from the Senate about 9:15 p.m., heard on his car radio that Stennis had been shot.

The attack first was reported as an assassination attempt, not a cheap street robbery. "I knew that there was nothing I could do medically," Hatfield related later to a Wheaton College audience (May 9, 1977). "I had no skills to offer. But I knew there was something I must do—and that was to go to that hospital and be nearby where I could be helpful, if possible, to the family."

Even though Hatfield and Stennis both belonged to a Wednesday morning Senate prayer group, they seemingly had little in common. As the original Vietnam "dove" in the Senate, Hatfield had clashed often and sharply with Stennis, a champion of the military. (The Mississippian's hawkish views moderated in the early 1970s, however.) Indeed, Hatfield himself says that the only senator with whom he disagreed more, politically, was Strom Thurmond of South Carolina.

"And yet I knew John Stennis, out of that relationship, to be a man who was committed to the Lord, who sought the Lord's will in his life," the Oregonian said. "I went to the hospital. . . . there was great, great confusion, and there was great stir because he was, and is, a nationally recognized leader."

The barrage of telephone calls and visits from news reporters, Senate colleagues, and curious friends overwhelmed the hospital's telephone operators. Officials set up a temporary office to field the questions. "It was very obvious that they were undermanned, and they were disorganized," Hatfield recalls. He spotted an unattended switchboard, sat down, and went to work.

Much later, after his recovery, Stennis related a second-hand version of what happened next: "He told the girls, 'I know how to work one of these; let me help you out.' He went to taking calls until daylight. Then he got up, and he put on his coat and said, 'My name is Hatfield, Senator Hatfield.' That characterizes the man. Always so willing to help."[3]

Hatfield, remembering the night, terms it an occasion when one doesn't think about what to do—he just does it:

> I knew if I gave my name out that there might be those who would recognize a political connection. . . . They would ask me, 'And who are you?' And I would say, 'My name is Mark

Odom' and pause, because those are my first two names. Not completely dishonest—just a little dishonest.

So we carried forth and then would go into the room where Mrs. Stennis was waiting for the reports from the surgery and try to be helpful, and my wife came to be helpful to Mrs. Stennis as well.

A very small, very insignificant action. And yet it was out of that that the word became known that I was involved, and the press couldn't quite handle it. It boggled their minds.

"How do you, as a liberal Republican, relate yourself in this way to a conservative Democrat?" they asked me. And I would say, "We may have our politics that vary and differ, but we are bound together by a stronger bond—our common commitment to the Lord."

That episode, which Senator Stennis often relates, tells much about the direction Mark Hatfield's life is taking. To a considerable extent in recent years, he has become a living example of the new way of life and spiritual direction he seeks for the United States and the church. Hatfield considers justice—compassion, fairness, and protection of human life—as the task of the nation and "relational religion"[4] as the mandate for the church. That refreshing perspective transcends the conventional conservatism-liberalism argument, as well as the evangelical split between preaching the gospel and social concern.

Hatfield's plea for a new spiritual direction is nowhere more evident than in his approach to America's bicentennial celebration. Unlike most politicians, he avoided virtually all expression of civil religion. His first bicentennial directive was to the church: "Our message is a radical revolution through Jesus Christ. . . . This is the new American revolution that would be greater, more earth-shaking, and more world-influencing than the revolution that followed the first Continental Congress two centuries ago."[5] He renewed his call (not limiting it to conservative evangelicals) at the 1976 National Prayer Breakfast:

To believe that true faithfulness to Jesus Christ will bolster our structures of power, or protect society's status quo is impious folly. We who are finite dare not attempt to use an infinite God for our own ends.

What we require . . . is a new revolution—a spiritual revolution transforming our values and shaping our corporate life. This would be the natural manifestation of true repentance.

Let us begin this revolution now. Let us be known as a people who are committed to the primacy of spiritual community, and as just and compassionate stewards in service to the needs of humanity.

Let us today covenant one with another to mobilize our resources and commit our lives for the corporate spiritual transformation which this revolution will bring.[6]

What might have been a proper bicentennial celebration? The senator suggested the biblical "Year of Jubilee" (Leviticus 25) as a model. Accordingly, he said, U.S. citizens should: (1) confess their national sins and make reconciliation with their global neighbors; (2) acknowledge their enslavement to institutions, cultural patterns, social status, and habits; (3) seek economic liberation by helping those in bondage to poverty; and (4) seek ecological liberation by following the old Hebrew principle of allowing the land to rest periodically and by living in harmony with the environment.

The senator's call for a new style of politics and his opposition to civil religion appeared again during the 1976 presidential election campaign. The three major candidates of both parties (Republicans Gerald Ford and Ronald Reagan, and Democrat Jimmy Carter) professed evangelical beliefs. Hatfield was uneasy with some implications from the candidates' statements and especially with the response of the secular media. Both media and candidates implied that religion is dualistic and narrow, a "guarantee of a candidate's morality and integrity, but not . . . the basis for one's social and political vision of society." The Oregonian's own fusion of faith and politics long ago had convinced him that "the gospel of Christ calls believers to a whole set of commitments, values, and lifestyles . . . which would inevitably have an influence on the decisions made by a politician who not only professed such a faith, but lived it."[7]

Hatfield suggested that all candidates who claim allegiance to Christ should commit themselves to: (1) standing for the poor and oppressed and against all exploiting institutions and social structures; (2) opposing all forms of violence and militancy, and even loving one's enemies; (3) opposing America's materialistic lifestyle; and (4) viewing political leadership as servanthood. The three candidates made no public response.

Since the bicentennial year, Hatfield has exhibited his radicalness in almost every area of politics, including the "human rights" issue of foreign policy. The senator agreed with President Carter's professed intention of making human rights a central theme in international relations. Unfortunately, Hatfield soon judged that the Carter Administration was wavering on human rights, choosing to apply the moral imperative only where it coincided with U.S. economic and strategic interests.

During the ninety-fifth Congress, Hatfield joined with Sen. James Abourezk, a Democrat from South Dakota, in an unsuccessful amendment which instructed U.S. financial representatives on international organizations to vote against granting loans to countries with consistent patterns of human rights violations. Abourezk admires Hatfield for "voting his conscience"[8] on pressure-packed questions.

Perhaps the best example of Hatfield's compassion and courage is his campaign for an international boycott of Ugandan coffee because of that nation's human rights violations. The senator labeled Uganda President Idi Amin Dada's leadership "rule by slaughter." Concerning Amin and his henchmen, Hatfield said: "The world has not seen such ferocious institutionalized brutality since the concentration camps of Stalin's Russia or Hitler's Reich."[9]

Republican Sen. Lowell Weicker, Jr., of Connecticut joined Hatfield in sponsoring legislation (which was successful) imposing a trade embargo against Ugandan coffee. The Oregon senator had hoped the embargo would lead to the downfall of Amin, because the Ugandan economy is heavily dependent on the sale of coffee to Western nations. To Hatfield, the move was more than moral rhetoric: "For those who would stereotype such a boycott as nothing more than a token display of moral outrage, I say that if ever there was a case where economic sanctions are likely to be effective, it is this one."

Another example of Hatfield's consistent concern for international justice is his position on the Panama Canal. Even though he faced reelection in 1978 (with opposition from conservatives), the senator spoke out forthrightly for gradual withdrawal from this "colonial enclave." He downplayed the significance of Panama's internal political situation, arguing that the United States should take the initiative, through bargaining and compromise, in dealing with the problem of Panamanian self-determination versus U.S. colonialism.

Said Hatfield: "Our exercise of jurisdiction in the Canal Zone does not change the fact that the most reliable way to guarantee a safe and open canal is by securing the consent and cooperation of the Panamanian people."[10] Only to the casual observer was Hatfield's position in the "liberal" camp; rather, his stance was logical in light of his foreign policy evolution.

The senator was one of the first legislators to fight development of radiation warheads for the so-called neutron bomb. He contends that such controlled weapons would make it easier for countries to justify using nuclear arms. Hatfield's military perspective evolved from the Vietnam experience and his avowed goal of preserving, not destroying, human life. Yet Senator Stennis believes that Hatfield is misunderstood. "He's very honest about it," Stennis says. "But he's not an extremist. No sir. I don't think he's what you might call anti-military."[11]

One Oregon reporter observes that Hatfield "is as much a critic of military spending as one can be and survive politically. His views on that subject are probably tolerable to someone like Stennis only because they carry little weight."[12] As a matter of principle, Hatfield and others like Senator McGovern have reached the point of almost annual protest votes against escalating military budgets. Hatfield doesn't confine his nays to the U.S. defense establishment, however; he opposes exporting war machinery, too. His consistency is demonstrated by votes against the sale of arms to *both* sides in the Mideast conflict.[13]

An important ingredient of Hatfield's foreign policy continues to be programs designed to bring relief to millions suffering from hunger and poverty. Unfortunately, official response to such problems seldom matched the senator's evaluation of the need.

On the domestic scene, the Oregonian reintroduced his neighborhood government and Simpliform bills. And he supported assorted legislation dealing with economic decentralization. In particular, he renewed his call for deregulation of the petroleum industry—figuring that was the route to greater productivity and more competition in alternate sources of energy.

In line with his concern for "people power" through decentralization and localism, Hatfield sponsored or supported legislation to (1) give greater voting rights to residents of the District of Columbia; (2) make third-party candidates eligible for public financing in Senate general elections (although still within the basic two-party framework); and (3) give tuition tax credits for college and vocational schools. (But he opposes efforts to extend such legislation to private and secondary schools.)

The senator's most creative and far-reaching proposal of late may be his call for a constitutional amendment to provide for a voter initiative on issues affecting the entire country. Senator Abourezk co-sponsored the plan, which would submit any legislative proposal to the people if 3 percent of all eligible voters in the previous presidential election signed petitions. Based on the 1976 election, that proposal would require petitions containing only about 2.5 million valid signatures. Since backers of California's 1978 Proposition 13—calling for lowered property taxes—collected more than 1.2 million signers in that state alone, it is apparent that the 3 percent figure is reachable. Hatfield considers the proposal a way to give people more control over their lives without creating social turmoil.

Hatfield's evolving radicalness has not undermined his effectiveness as a senator. Despite his concern about the responsiveness of the system, he has won several victories for Oregon interests (particularly in the area of public works). "There's a certain quid pro quo in the system, and it goes beyond appropriations..." Hatfield told a *Portland Oregonian* reporter (October 29, 1978).

"There are a lot of things in the system I don't like. In the meantime, here the system is, and we have to make the best of it."

A vital factor in Hatfield's accomplishment in the Senate (in addition to membership on the important Appropriations and Energy and Natural Resources Committees) is the esteem with which he is held by other senators. One example is the conservative Stennis. But Hatfield also has excellent working relationships with such relatively liberal—and powerful—Democrats as Frank Church of Idaho and William Proxmire of Wisconsin. Today the Oregon senator seemingly can wear many hats and work in many circles without compromising basic Christian principles.

Recently Hatfield has become more convinced than ever that the church should be viewed as a *body*, a living organism, rather than as a collection of isolated individuals. His model for this organism is the New Testament church, a fellowship of "enduring love, interdependence, stability, loyalty, devotion, commitment, responsibility, and security in time of crisis...."[14] Individuals, then, find their meaning as they relate one to another within this vibrant community.

The senator continues to call for members of this body to follow the pattern of Jesus, the suffering servant, the one who rejected political power and made himself vulnerable for the sake of the world:

> We have been inculturated to believe that one who really has power somehow exercises it by imposing his will, by commanding the situation in a way that others must yield and subjugate themselves. And here was Christ, the leader, the servant, the liberator. This to me is the unique message that Christians have to offer all institutions of power.[15]

The key to understanding Hatfield's perspective comes not from the definitions themselves, for they are refinements of previous statements, but in their foundation. To the senator, true discipleship seems to mean *exemplarism*—in this case, copying the life and witness of Jesus and the New Testament church. Since Jesus is the model, only by tracing the pattern of his earthly ministry can his followers become biblical (or political) leaders in the pure sense.

To protect the integrity of the church, the senator reacted sharply when reports circulated in 1975 and 1976 that the U.S. Central Intelligence Agency used missionaries as agents. This type of foreign policy, Hatfield believes, is a violation of New Testament teachings. "It is one of the fundamental principles of our society that the church is not an arm of the state . . ." he wrote in *Christian Herald* ("Missionaries and the CIA," March 1976). Further, the state must be restrained "from its tendency to seek a presumed end through dubious means."

The senator translated his outrage into legislation prohibiting any connection—whether just collecting information or engaging in clandestine activities—between the CIA and clergy or missionaries. At first the CIA and White House leaders resisted such a change but, to Hatfield's satisfaction, the leadership later retreated and halted the CIA-missionary interaction.

Such "politicizing" of the church is only one of several important themes Hatfield touched on in an interview published in the April 1976 issue of *Vanguard* magazine.[16] In that article the senator says "we are the church dispersed," a dynamic fellowship called to remain as open and nonstructured as possible. Hence, "I feel that we become too programme-oriented and therefore we begin to fail to really let flow the greatest power [of love] we could."

So much emphasis on structure and program in the church is a sign of danger to Hatfield:

> You see, when you begin to institutionalize the word "christian," including the church, when it becomes an institutional vehicle to mobilize for other purposes, you run great dangers. And you begin to find not only the character of the institution coming under challenge as to whether it is christian or nonchristian. But I think you begin to see it affecting the very major and exclusive thrust of the church—to proclaim the gospel . . . the total gospel, message and mission.

The clear traces of what might be called "anti-institutionalism" in that statement are not surprising, coming from the author of neighborhood government legislation.

The senator extends that anti-institutionalism, as he had in

earlier years, to "Christian" politics à la the European model.
While he acknowledges that the Christian Democrats of West
Germany, for example, are a viable political party, he questions
whether they are "Christian" as such. He suggests there are no
criteria upon which to judge such parties. What about the need for
Christian political organizations in the United States?

> I think there's always a need for clearinghouses of informa-
> tion, for Christians to have a dependable and scholarly type
> of daily material. And so for clearinghouse types of organiza-
> tions, yes. Now if you're talking about a political party, no.
> NO. Absolutely, irretrievably, no. I think this would be
> disastrous. I think that it would be unscriptural. I just shud-
> der to think about a Christian party.

In this statement, as much as anywhere, the shaping power of
both the historic Baptist movement and radical Anabaptism on the
senator's politics are most evident.

As an alternative to forming distinct Christian political parties,
Hatfield advises Christians to infiltrate existing structures with the
"virus of love," relating, sharing, and binding up personal wounds.
Such infiltration might create

> a Christian caucus in the existing institution. . . . You've seen
> as well as I have where a small minority band of people who
> were really tied together could overthrow a majority within
> the framework of the free and nonviolent vehicles open to
> them. I've never known, for instance, a political party orga-
> nization at the county level that couldn't be taken over by de-
> termined and committed people who really wanted to do it.

The senator's call for infiltration has not been heeded by progressive evangelicals. As a body they remain mildly apathetic, largely
content with the system and individualistic in their politics. Ironically, this is not the case with those of the political far right within
conservative Christianity. Thanks to the nature of the political
system and apathy of the American people, the right-wing faction is
capitalizing on the infiltration idea.

Oregon is a case in point. In 1978, fundamentalist preacher
Walter Huss—who opposed Hatfield in the 1966 Senate primary

election—captured the state's Republican Party chairmanship. Huss first attracted public notice in the late 1950s by speaking out against the menace of communism. In 1966 he challenged Governor Hatfield on the governor's "dovish" Vietnam stand. Hatfield easily defeated Huss, who also lost a 1968 bid for a U.S. House nomination. From 1968 until 1978 Huss and his wife, Rosalie, had been heard from only sporadically, as they worked chiefly at the county political level.

Huss followed Hatfield's infiltration formula when engineering the 1978 party takeover (Huss supporters won other offices, too). The fundamentalist minister organized fellow conservative Christians at the local level, then built upon that base all the way to the state convention. As a result, though, Hatfield and most other Republican candidates for major offices unofficially created individual reelection committees—thereby disassociating themselves from their own state organization.

Many Republican leaders reacted harshly to the Huss brand of politics, which included a statement that the chairman would like Republican candidates to be Christians because they tend to act morally. Hatfield, however, ignored Huss until late October when the party chairman challenged the senator's declaration that the military budget could be slashed without endangering national security.

Huss asked how the nation could "develop a national will to oppose the Soviet superpower when you penetrate the minds of people with this doctrine of pacifism?" In good radical Anabaptist fashion Hatfield replied: "My trust in the future is not vested in military hardware. . . ." Other nations fell, the senator said, because "they pursued the false gods of materialism."[17]

That campaign clash with Huss probably confirmed Hatfield's suspicions of Christian (or church) politics, making it unlikely that he ever will lead a distinct Christian political movement. Nor is he likely even to direct an infiltration of the present two-party system by the progressive evangelical community. That is unfortunate—should the progressives leave both options exclusively to the conservatives?

Apart from the Huss confrontation, Oregon's 1978 Senate election was uneventful. Hatfield's Democratic challenger, State Sen. Vern Cook, mounted a vigorous campaign, but he was a substantial underdog from the beginning. Even though Oregon Democrats still outnumber Republicans, Hatfield won a third Senate term by a comfortable margin.

What conclusions can be drawn about Hatfield's remarkable thirty years of political service? The mature expression of his unique Christian politics—an amalgamation of radical Anabaptism, neo-Hooverism, and neo-evangelicalism—deserves acclaim on several counts:

First, Hatfield's radical politics penetrates to the root of America's spiritual and political malaise in many areas. His is an integral, holistic politics, rallying the church and individual Christians against many forms of dualism—especially the traditional separation of mission and message, evangelism and social concern, church and state.

Second, the senator's politics is prophetic, allowing him to call for a Christian stance of countercultural "over-againstness" to political and economic oppression, civil religion, and materialism. At the same time, prophetic Christianity undergirds his appeal for identification with the poor, stewardship of natural resources, and national repentance for past wrongdoings.

Third, he realizes that human government is a limited institution, whose major goal is to provide justice by allowing the greatest possible expression of freedom for individuals and for small, decentralized communities. In short, Hatfield transcends conventional liberal politics which relies on the cultural impetus of a powerful national government, and conservative politics because of his plea for economic as well as political decentralization.

Fourth, Hatfield is emerging as a unique moral leader— stressing compassion, "relationships," and servanthood—at a time when moral leadership is sorely lacking. Older concepts of political power are coming under sharp criticism; America needs a leader with Hatfield's ethical vision.

Even though the senator is a statesman almost without comparison on the American political horizon, he is not a saint, nor does he claim to be. Hatfield does not have all the political answers. There are some basic weaknesses in his perspective.

First, his world view, although radical and holistic, is too theologically oriented. He is influenced by radical Anabaptist and (neo) evangelical theologians rather than by Christian political theorists. Hence comes his definition of the church as an "organism" and his anti-institutionalism. But the church is more than a loose organism, a nonstructured fellowship. It is a body which needs as many organizational forms as there are organized tasks to perform.

The senator has moved slowly toward theological pacifism. If he continues in that direction, he will find it increasingly difficult to distinguish between individual (or church) love and "political" love. Such a distinction is necessary simply because the state, although a real entity, is not an individual and cannot love like an individual. While a state is also called to give loving service to God, the state cannot respond like an individual. Love for the state means the authoritative implementation of justice, not turning the other cheek.

Hatfield, too, must avoid the pitfalls of theological exemplarism, specifically basing political action on the model of Jesus and the New Testament church. Exemplarism which goes beyond the realm of attitude and principle can be dangerous. Christians today engage in many actions which are foreign to Jesus and the early church, yet they are necessary to be effective servants. The question "What would Jesus *do*?" is not as relevant as "What would Jesus *have us do*?"

Second, the call to a prophetic, countercultural Christianity can be misconstrued, leading to withdrawal from society and failure to develop positive political and economic alternatives for the system. Unfortunately this has happened to some radical Christian communities. Though Hatfield seems aware of this danger, he nonetheless encourages an attitude of withdrawal by pleading for Christians to stand "over-against" the political establishment. His prophetic Christianity needs something more positive in a structural sense—more positive, even, than his own creative call for political and economic decentralization.

Third, the lack of a complementary element is evident in the senator's philosophy of the state and politics. While stimulating and refreshing, his view of the positive role of the state is so constricted that his assessment of conventional politics almost becomes an "anti-politics." For example, his neighborhood government legislation is hampered because he is reluctant to tackle the problem of minimum national standards for small communities. Establishing minimums requires a positive theory of the state, which Hatfield largely lacks. Apparently he associates such a theory with modern political liberalism.

Another shortcoming is his narrow, basically geographical definition of community. His program of localism doesn't make room for religious, ethnic, or ideological groups to participate equally with geographical communities. This narrowness contributes to his suspicion of a distinct Christian political movement. Hatfield, as well as other radical Anabaptists, has yet to show convincingly why Christians should not band together politically. Does he believe that God will honor united efforts elsewhere—but not in politics?

Fourth, the senator needs to assume a more forceful role as a distinctly *political* leader alongside his unquestioned role as a prophetic moral leader. Until he and other insightful leaders move in this direction, authentic cultural pluralism in America will remain a dream.

Finally, Hatfield needs to become solidly anchored in (Christian) political theory and less issue-oriented and pragmatic. Even during the last decade or two—the pinnacle of his radical politics—he has *reacted* to situations more than he has marched ahead with a framework already in hand. One place in which he could begin to search for complementary models would be by investigating Christian political theories within Reformed circles, especially the Dutch Calvinist tradition.[18] Fusion of radical Anabaptist and Reformed perspectives could provide more theoretical depth and practical breadth to the senator's unconventional politics.

What about the future for Hatfield? "More of the same" is the likely answer, and that is not bad. He is highly regarded among politicians despite his radicalism. He has steadily gained seniority among Republicans, and he is a competent legislator for the state of Oregon.

His acceptance can be seen partly as the result of his definition of politics as an "exercise in human relations." His whole program is built upon "relational" religion and politics. He earnestly seeks to build bridges of interpersonal communication, to tear down walls of suspicion and animosity so prevalent among politicians and between political parties. A clear example of this is the Stennis episode. Even Democratic Rep. Robert Duncan, Hatfield's 1966 senatorial opponent and sharp critic, acknowledges that the senator has become an effective legislator. The two men today have a cordial relationship.

Hatfield attributes much of his effectiveness and personal security to the strength of his family life (as well as to the bonds of personal friendship). "I feel strongly that my political philosophy and my whole public life is really geared not only to reflect my trust in Christ but my love for my family," the senator says. Following Hoover, Hatfield considers the family the "cornerstone of the republic"; a deteriorating family structure means political and cultural suicide for any nation.

After the family come other personal friendships. He suggests that it would have been impossible to continue his radical brand of politics without the rock-like support of his friends. Personal strength as a Christian, then, comes to Hatfield first in the context of his family and then as part of his fellowship in the Christian community.

Because the senator experiences God's love through family and friendships, he has largely conquered his own political ambition. There have been times—1968, for instance—when he coveted higher office; such is not the case today. He is content to be a U.S. senator from Oregon: "I have no ambition beyond the position I'm in. Further, I have a totally freewheeling attitude toward the whole political circumstance in which I find myself. I'm very loose about it." That self-assessment is confirmed by his closest associates.

One final theme of the mature Hatfield remains: He wants to be more than a good senator, more than a radical legislator who designs reform proposals like Simpliform and the Neighborhood

Government Act. His dream of late has been to help guide the evangelical community out of the social and political desert where he feels it has been wandering so much of this century:

> I have more recently felt that perhaps my desire, if I'm to leave an impact, would be to be a stimulant or a catalyst or some vehicle by which we relate the Christian community more into an active role in government; whereby the moral dimension . . . would be more apparent in the decision-making process of our government. If somehow I could, in whatever tenure I spend here as a senator, have created a greater awareness within the Christian community, for a meaningful role . . . that they could be active, I feel that would be the greatest contribution I could make.

Thus, Senator Hatfield wants first to be a political prophet to his own "country," his own people—a lonely role that frequently is frustrating but which also can be immensely rewarding. The senator has earned his stripes on the political battlefront. In so many ways fellow evangelicals, whether they agree with him or not, recognize that all along the lonesome path he has been "our senator."

Epilogue

TO GLIMPSE the present perspective of Senator Mark Hatfield, one needs only to examine an interview with him entitled "The Illusion of Arms Control," appearing in the February 1979 issue of *Sojourners* magazine. His contemporary radicalism and transcendence .can be seen clearly—and they can be contrasted with the conventional wisdom of America's political system and with key elements of American Christianity.

President Carter's administration believes that the SALT II strategic arms limitation treaty with the Soviet Union is crucial to detente and the future of world peace. Hatfield, however, is suspicious, fearing that it would move the United States in precisely the wrong direction—*away* from real disarmament and a lessening of international tensions. His fear is based on two observations: (1) Many present weapons systems, and those now being developed, apparently will be exempt. The cruise missile and the massive new Trident II missile are examples. (2) Many future sophisticated weapons systems will not be mentioned in the document. Such systems include hunter-killer satellites, particle-beam weapons, and "terminal guidance" weapons. In this latter category are devices which will give the United States (a nation which supposedly has a defensive posture) much greater first-strike capability, thus increasing tension with the Soviets and, inevitably, pushing them toward sophisticated countermeasures.

Hatfield views this trend with alarm: "Everything seems to be an escalation of madness, an insanity of self-destruction." And he is increasingly disturbed at the "official line" coming from the administration and from political and religious leaders in general. Just because we repeatedly call something a "strategic arms limitation treaty" does not make it so, he observes. Ultimately, he believes, SALT II is deceptive and harmful to America's future prospects:

> [SALT II] confuses matters. It confuses a public which believes we are getting some kind of real constriction or stabilization of our nuclear arsenals. And that's misleading. Because of this confusion, some real and valid arms control program—one that could be built on a clear determination that we're going to limit and reduce military expenditures and nuclear weapons—is made impossible.
>
> . . . we aren't really getting much of anything except the political, ceremonial event of signing a document.
>
> . . . That's why I feel very strongly that at this point we ought to be about the business of SALT III—making a commitment to achieve a real limit and reduction of these ongoing programs, and addressing ourselves to the forthcoming weapons. Getting public understanding and support for such an approach to arms control now would be a far more significant development than misleading the public into thinking that we have achieved something which is actually illusory.

Hatfield recommends that SALT II "fade out" and be forgotten; America should move directly to a treaty with real substance.

Hatfield's outspoken approach to SALT II is shared by such "liberals" as Senators McGovern and Proxmire. The three expressed their objections in a letter to President Carter in March 1979. Ironically, the trio appears to join forces with the political right—including evangelical conservatives—in opposing SALT II. However, conservative evangelicals no doubt oppose the treaty because they believe it will lead to disarmament at a time when greater military strength is needed—hardly the Hatfield-McGovern-Proxmire approach.

On the other hand, the reputedly liberal Hatfield opposes other political and Christian liberals who support SALT II. To his political friends he implies that traditional labels are not meaningful today. To the liberal Christian community he boldly asserts that they are "buying a false package, a false hope" in supporting the treaty. It is of small consequence to him if he appears to take contradictory actions in the eyes of the political or religious establishments. This attitude reflects a unique transcendence of conventional labels and polarities.

Hatfield's transcendence is clearly evident when he shares his personal Christian beliefs and evaluates the role of the church on disarmament. The senator says his own perspective is based on the Christian concept of *creation* (it ought not be destroyed, for it belongs to God); *stewardship* (administering creation for all its inhabitants); *reconciliation* (uniting by imitating Christ, not separating people: "The more armaments you build which separate people, threaten people, and cause fear . . . the more you deny the Christian commission of reconciliation."); and *sharing* (compassionately giving of our resources to others). These biblical principles are perhaps more uniquely fused and forcefully articulated by radical Anabaptists today than by many others.

Hatfield further declares that the church has failed to speak out against the arms race because it has "reflected the cultural values and the political priorities of society rather than heeding the call to become a subculture. I think that the Christian community in this secular, materialistic age is increasingly going to have to be seen and understood as a subculture, or a counterculture." The senator yearns for Christian "resistance" and "counteraction," but he sees only church resolutions and proposals, most of which support the present approach to arms control. Says Hatfield: "I am weary of resolutions."

Again, these Hatfield themes reflect a biblical Christianity which corresponds most closely (although not exclusively) to the broad outlines of radical Anabaptism. His "answer," too, presents this type of message:

> I would much rather see the life of the people of the church demonstrate. . . their values as Christians, and their confidence in God as . . . the source of their security. That would do far more to influence the political institutions than passing a resolution.
>
> We must exemplify in our lives the Christian gospel. . . . We must act as lambs being sent into a world of

wolves. On the surface, that seems like idiocy. But there is in this approach the power of God. . . .

So the question becomes, can the church simply be the church? . . . Where will we place our trust? In our nation's armaments, or in our Lord?

Until the church is willing to assume a truly countercultural role in proclaiming an alternative basis of security and trust in its own life—a life marked by love and reconciliation—I don't think it will have much of an effective role in the question of disarmament.

Or in anything else. . . .

Appendix:
Christian Socio-Political
Organizations

SEN. MARK HATFIELD is only one of the many Christians holding public office throughout North America. Others at the U.S. national level include President Jimmy Carter, Rep. John Anderson (Rep.-Illinois), newly elected Sen. William Armstrong (Rep.-Colorado), Sen. John Stennis (Dem.-Mississippi), and newly elected Gov. Albert Quie (Rep.-Minnesota). At regional and local levels, and in Canada, hundreds of others could be named. Hatfield and other Christian politicians covet the prayers and thoughtful support of their Christian brethren.

Supporting individual politicians, however, is only one option open to Christians. Within the past few years another avenue for evangelical political expression has emerged—socio-political organizations which seek to unite Christians into fairly distinct associations or communities. This is difficult in a nation where individualism is a pervasive force and where "religious" politics is suspect. Even Christian politicians are initially suspicious of socio-political movements proclaiming to be "Christian." Such a dilemma exists because of the reductionistic world views of these political leaders, resulting from decades of politics conducted in a vacuum (created by Christian separation from organized political activity). Hence, our legacy is a political *system* largely shaped by the force of secularism.

In reaction to this spirit and its resulting political distortions, and as a positive expression of a more holistic interpretation of the Gospel, the following organizations have been formed:

ASSOCIATION FOR PUBLIC JUSTICE

Born in 1977, the Association for Public Justice (APJ) is the heir of an organization formed in the mid-1960s (most recently called the National Association for Christian Political Action). Although it is an evangelical organization open to all, much of its support initially came from Reformed circles. APJ draws, for example, upon the historical resources of Dutch (Kuyperian) Calvinism—a source rich in Christian political witness. This partly accounts for a distinct political confession and theoretical foundation.

Few organizations have such concise, biblically sensitive political beliefs. Paraphrased, these beliefs are that (1) Christ is Lord of politics, delegating authority directly to various human institutions; (2) the state is the legal community of public justice; (3) government is the office of human authority within the state, which should have free and fair elections open to all adult citizens; (4) government should distribute goods and services to all, without prejudice against anyone's religion; (5) government should not infringe upon the sovereign spheres of other human institutions or individuals but should enhance them by providing justice; (6) no one should be compelled to accept any political creed by any government, person, or institution, including APJ. Perhaps these beliefs can best be summarized as "principled pluralism."

APJ is a nonchurch, voluntary association organized to implement God's norm of justice for all. It does not seek special status for itself or for evangelical Christians. Presently, APJ has three goals: (1) to build a grass roots political movement through education and organization; (2) to expand research and policy studies among specially trained evangelicals, moving in the direction of establishing a Christian political research center; (3) to serve politicians at all levels by sharing research and proposals with them.

To fulfill these goals, APJ does all of the following: publishes a monthly newsletter, holds annual international conferences, assigns research projects to analytical teams, conducts summer political institutes at various Christian colleges, drafts position papers (for example, "Justice in Education"), sponsors books (a book is forthcoming on educational justice in the United States), creates regional action committees, and prepares testimony for governmental committees (recently testimony was given before House and Senate committees on the Tuition Tax Credit legislation).

APJ does not sponsor candidates for public office nor is it a political party, although the organization doesn't preclude such options for the future. Organization leaders wish to remain open to many kinds of political action. For further information (about membership, principles, publications, conferences, etc.) contact John Hulst (president), Box 5769, Washington, D.C. 20014.

COMMITTEE FOR JUSTICE AND LIBERTY

North of the border in Ontario, Canada, there is an organization of kindred spirit to APJ, the Committee for Justice and Liberty (CJL). Both organizations have common historical roots in Dutch Calvinism, although CJL, too, offers membership to all who accept its principles and vision.

CJL, which was incorporated in April 1963, is one of the oldest Christian political organizations still functioning. Like APJ, CJL principles are basically Reformed—stressing the Lordship of Christ over all life, including politics, and the necessity of communal political service by Christians (guided by the biblical concepts of "stewardship" of natural resources and "public justice.") For several years the association pondered the best ways to express socio-political principles, gain supporters, and select and research national issues about which to formulate policy statements. By the early 1970s, CJL had enrolled hundreds of new members and difficult years of research and analysis were bearing fruit.

Since CJL is a voluntary association and not, at present, a political party, most recent efforts have been directed toward political lobbying at Canadian provincial and national boards of inquiry and legislative committees. The association has become one of the most effective "religious" pressure groups, also gaining the acceptance, as a co-belligerent, of similar organizations in Canada.

Success can be attributed partly to choosing the right issues—

national energy policy and economic development of the Canadian Northwest Territories. CJL has presented testimony to appropriate committees and has even fought successful legal battles all the way to the Canadian Supreme Court.

In the energy field, the association's plea is for a new Canadian lifestyle that consumes less energy and is more responsive to all creatures and institutions, not just to profit-seeking corporations. CJL wants the Northwest Territories to be opened up without irreparable harm to native culture and the fragile environment. They demand that committees and boards concentrating on these issues represent the diverse viewpoints within Canada's pluralistic society.

CJL publishes *Catalyst*, a quarterly in-depth newsletter, sponsors conferences, and participates in discussions about Canada's political future. No other organization in North America has more potential for exerting system-transforming force at regional or national levels. To obtain more information, including what support U.S. citizens can give, contact Gerald Vandezande, executive director, CJL Foundation, 229 College Street, Toronto, Ontario M5T1R4.

EVANGELICALS FOR SOCIAL ACTION

In November 1973 more than 50 prominent evangelical leaders gathered in Chicago, Illinois, for a conference on social concern and justice. After several days of deliberation, they issued the "Chicago Declaration," which was immediately recognized as a watershed proclamation for evangelicalism. Even more liberal magazines like *Christian Century* and the secular press acknowledged that evangelicals might be on the brink of a new social and political consciousness if this declaration were more than pious rhetoric.

The declaration was a radical and prophetic call to biblical living wherein evangelicals declared the Lordship of Christ over life, confessed their own sinful shortcomings in the areas of social concern and recognition of national injustice, attacked materialism and the exploitation of the poor, and demanded that righteousness and justice be the norm for America and her people. [For details see Ron Sider (ed.), *The Chicago Declaration* (Carol Stream, Illinois: Creation House, 1974).]

The national evangelical movement started by this declaration *is* more than pious rhetoric. The conference was followed by informal discussions and by annual workshops on social issues, leading to substantive papers and stronger bonds of evangelical fellowship and commitment. In 1977 leaders decided that a permanent organization was necessary to carry out the vision and principles born in Chicago. By September 1978 a skeletal framework had been established for Evangelicals for Social Action (ESA).

ESA's purpose is to (1) educate evangelicals on issues of justice; (2) establish a clearinghouse for information, resources, and projects; (3) establish a network of support for isolated evangelicals at the local level; and (4) initiate social action projects.

To reach these goals—with a small staff and limited budget—ESA is establishing local chapters, initiating national justice and issue-oriented task forces, organizing a consultation on evangelism and justice, publishing a newsletter, organizing conferences for pastors at evangelical seminaries, printing "Tracts for Justice," and sponsoring a national congress on social justice, planned for 1981.

Of the voluntary associations listed in this survey, ESA has perhaps the greatest potential for ecumenical evangelical support in the United States. As a solidly evangelical and slightly Anabaptistic organization it also is somewhat more social and humanitarian than political, although it may take on a more prophetic political "witness" in the future. Unlike APJ and CJL, though, there is little probability that ESA will even consider becoming a political party or an exclusively political movement. The influences of Anabaptism and general American evangelicalism rule out this option.

More information is available from Todd Putney, coordinator, Evangelicals for Social Action, 300 West Apsley Street, Philadelphia, Pennsylvania 19144.

DUNAMIS

In the early 1970s a small group associated with the dynamic

Church of the Savior in Washington, D.C., started a prophetic political "ministry." They called the new mission "Dunamis," the Greek word for power—the power of being led by God's Spirit as in the day of Pentecost. Dunamis leaders soon discovered that other evangelical Christians were being prepared by God for a political ministry in which Dunamis would take the lead.

Dunamis originally operated under a council representing primarily the Washington vicinity. Now, with the emergence of several Dunamis movements throughout the United States, there is a board with representatives from many areas. Among its various activities, the District of Columbia office edits a newsletter and sponsors "institutes," or seminar-retreats, to discuss issues in depth.

For the first few years Dunamis searched for a meaningful phrase that would capture the essence of its ministry. Such a phrase, "Pastor-Prophets," was found in Senator Hatfield's "Pastors and Prophets" address at Princeton Seminary in 1974. Hence, the Dunamis program fuses the pastoral (caring for the salvation and personal wholeness of individuals) and the prophetic (standing against injustice on particular issues and with the poor and oppressed).

Members are encouraged to relate lovingly on one-to-one bases to governmental leaders. Three other principles are promulgated: (1) praying for political leaders, especially about specific issues; (2) growing in the Spirit in order to have a more effective ministry and to be better able to confront evil; (3) advocating for the poor and oppressed and building bridges between the poor and the rich.

A Dunamis member, after recognizing a problem, commits himself to becoming a part of the solution—praying at least fifteen minutes a day for the governmental unit concerned with the problem, gaining practical knowledge of the problem area, attending hearings or committee meetings, contacting one committee member (to share insights with and help this person), having fellowship with and gaining support from other evangelicals, and continuing in serious study of Scripture.

Dunamis, a voluntary social and humanitarian association, is shaped, in part, by the forces of Anabaptism and American individualism. Further information can be obtained from Marian Franz, 320 East Capitol Street, Washington, D.C. 20003.

CHRISTIANS FOR URBAN JUSTICE

In 1968 a handful of evangelicals recognized the desperate plight of urban minorities in Boston, Massachusetts, after the assassination of Martin Luther King. To address economic and political injustice they formed an organization called the Evangelical Committee for Urban Ministries in Boston (ECUMB). The committee published *Inside* magazine and sought to mobilize evangelicals toward developing community-based self-help programs, encouraging Christians to share resources for urban ministries, educating Christians about the nature of inner-city racism and the need for structural change, and opposing forces which oppress the poor.

In 1976 ECUMB shifted gears and entered a new phase of ministry under the name Christians for Urban Justice (CUJ). They terminated *Inside* magazine, partly because members felt *Inside* was duplicating efforts by magazines like *Sojourners* and *The Other Side* in alerting evangelicals to inner-city problems. CUJ concentrated more on practical Christian living in an urban setting where a new lifestyle would lead to community and concrete examples of structural political change. Presently CUJ is developing a dynamic community of evangelicals living and working with the poor in Dorchester, near Boston.

CUJ established a People Bank, providing funds for urban youth and for college and seminary scholarships. The organization sponsors a summer internship under which evangelical college students are trained in inner-city ministries. CUJ has also established an emergency relief fund to offset spiraling costs for rent and utilities and is beginning a drug and alcohol referral clinic at a local hospital.

For a time CUJ seemed to be successfully developing a Christian political newsletter of both national and regional focus. After months of work, however, lack of funds forced CUJ to postpone the newsletter project.

The organization's open membership has an ecumenical foundation. For example, the influence of historic Anabaptism is balanced by the forces of Reformed and progressive evangelical Christianity. CUJ appears to have potential for significant political witness in the near future, at least at the local-regional level. To discover more about the organization, write to Roger Dewey, Coordinator, Christians for Urban Justice, 598 Columbia Road, Dorchester, Massachusetts 02125.

SOJOURNERS FELLOWSHIP

In 1972 the appearance of a new publication, *Post American*, startled the evangelical world. To some it came as a breath of fresh air; to others it was subversive. *Post American* was the literary expression of the People's Christian Coalition—a small group of dissatisfied Chicago seminarians and Young Turks who were coalescing against many evils of American society and who opposed the civil religion of mainstream evangelicals. From the beginning, a version of radical Anabaptism was the dominant shaping force of the movement.

During the early 1970s, working in the Chicago area, the People's Coalition carried out a ministry of publication, speeches, dialogues, nonviolent protests, and attempts to build a vital Christian community. In 1975 self-evaluation led the small community to relocate in Washington, D.C. Now the coalition is called Sojourners Fellowship and the magazine is *Sojourners*.

The basic purposes of the movement remain the same: (1) a communal life built upon the model of the (local) New Testament church; (2) outreach to the church at large through the magazine and through traveling and raising issues basic to American society; and (3) a life of fellowship with and ministry to the poor.

In the early years, issues propelling the movement included opposition to the Vietnam War, irresponsible use of power by multinational economic corporations, and the socio-economic exploitation of the world's poor. Similar issues are still alive but two other subjects seem more important—human rights and nuclear arms. Nearly every issue of *Sojourners* includes prophetic denunciation of nuclear power and the arms race, as well as condemnation of human rights violations by nations (especially those on the political right). The fellowship has two packets of material summarizing the thinking of many members: "The Nuclear Challenge to Christian Conscience: A Study Guide for Churches" and "Seeds of the Kingdom: A Reader on Discipleship and the Shape of the Church."

Sojourners Fellowship is engaged in a different and, members believe, a more biblical kind of politics. The organization doesn't seek mass support to form a political lobby or political party. Rather, it is a community *living* politics according to the New Testament pattern. Members are convinced that, in the long run, only this approach will bring about meaningful structural change in the political system.

Their radical Anabaptist perspective makes Sojourners' members suspicious of calls—from right or left—for distinct Christian political movements within the present political system. An example of the *Sojourners* magazine perspective on right-wing Christian politics is found in their "expose" (April 1976) of conservative movements, entitled "The Plan to Save America: A Disclosure of an Alarming Political Initiative by the Evangelical Far Right."

For specific information about Sojourners Fellowship, contact Jim Wallis, editor, *Sojourners*, 1309 L Street Northwest, Washington, D.C. 20005.

Notes

Chapter 1 "Ratting on America"

[1]*Eternity*, 22 (July 1971), p. 4.
[2]Mark O. Hatfield, *Not Quite So Simple* (New York: Harper & Row, 1968), p. 159.
[3]Ibid., p. 161.
[4]Ibid., p. 163.
[5]Interview with Leolyn Barnett.

Chapter 2 Beginnings

[1]Milton MacKaye, "Oregon's Golden Boy," *Saturday Evening Post*, 231 (May 1959), p. 103.
[2]Mark Hatfield, *Between a Rock and a Hard Place* (Waco: Word Books, 1976), p. 111.
[3]Hatfield quoted in Herb Jauchen, "Statehouse Christian," *Christian Life*, 20 (January 1959), p. 12.
[4]MacKaye, "Oregon's Golden Boy," p. 104.

Chapter 3 Peeling Back the Veneer

[1]*Oregon State College Barometer*, October 26, 1951.
[2]Mark Hatfield, "The Truly Satisfying Life," *American Mercury*, 90 (June 1960), p. 61.
[3]Hatfield, "Committed to an Ideal," *Collegiate Challenge*, 1 (October 1961), p. 5.
[4]First paragraph: Hatfield, "Committed to an Ideal," p. 5. Second paragraph: Hatfield, "The Truly Satisfying Life," p. 62.
[5]*Medford Mail-Tribune*, February 23, 1955.
[6]Hatfield, *Not Quite So Simple*, p. 29.
[7]*Dallas Polk County Itemizer-Observer*, April 11, 1954.
[8]Hatfield, *Not Quite So Simple*, pp. 1-2.
[9]Ibid., p. 89.
[10]*Corvallis Gazette-Times*, April 7, 1954.

[11]His commitment to the Republican Party was strong but no unqualified. "I am not a party man, and I say that with pride," Hatfield told the *Portland Oregonian* (November 1, 1956). "I put the welfare of the public ahead of party loyalty."

Chapter 4   A Growing Christian Faith

[1]*Little Rock* (Arkansas) *American Baptist*, January 1958.

[2]Harold John Ockenga, "Resurgent Evangelical Leadership," *Christianity Today*, 5 (October 10, 1960), p. 11.

[3]Mark Hatfield, "The World's Appeal for Help," *The Alliance Witness*, 95 (August 10, 1960), p. 15.

[4]Hatfield statement, "What Christ Means to Me," c. 1960, p. 1.

[5]Hatfield, "Committed to an Ideal," p. 5.

[6]Newspaper reporters during these years frequently called him a "loner," "calculating," and an "enigma." One friend recalls Hatfield saying this about other politicians: "If a man ever double-crosses you, don't ever give him a second chance."

[7]See *New York Times*, November 4, 1958, p. 18, and A. Robert Smith, *Tiger in the Senate* (New York: Doubleday, 1962), pp. 370-379. Also see MacKaye, "Oregon's Golden Boy," pp. 32-33, 103-104, 106.

[8]*Salem Capital Journal*, October 10, 1958. For one critical article on Hatfield's religion, see Ralph Friedman, "Oregon: Scene of Strange Campaign," *The Progressive*, 22 (November 1958), pp. 39-41.

[9]Ibid. *Salem Capital Journal*.

[10]*Newberg Graphic*, June 6, 1957.

[11]Hatfield, "The Christian is Needed in Public Service," *Baptist Outlook*, 10 (Winter 1959), p. 6.

[12]Hatfield, "The World's Appeal for Help," p. 3.

Chapter 5   Oregon's Political Enigma

[1]Hatfield, *Not Quite So Simple*, pp. 39-40.

[2]Ibid., pp. 47 and 49.

[3]*Speeches of Governor Hatfield*, Vol. 1, No. 1, "The Role of the States," November 17, 1959, p. 1.

[4]*Medford Mail-Tribune*, September 19, 1962.

[5]Hatfield, *Between a Rock and a Hard Place*, p. 110. For an example of how Hatfield's philosophy has changed through the years, see his later assessment of this decision in chapter eleven.